SYLVIE FLEURY

DOUBLE POSITIVE

jrp|editions

Vivienne Westwood's *On Liberty* Fall/Winter 1994/95 collection succeeds her tartan masterstroke *Anglomania* collection, her signature interrogation of British historicism. *On Liberty* continues this project through abstracted padded bustles and equestrian riding coats, to which this piece responds. A black velvet coat lined in sheepskin shearling references the tailored vented 19th-century riding coat through a looser A-line silhouette. The collection's title, referring to John Stuart Mill's book of the same name, speaks to Westwood's design philosophy: the pursuit of individual style through the rubric of historical pastiche.

Matthew Linde

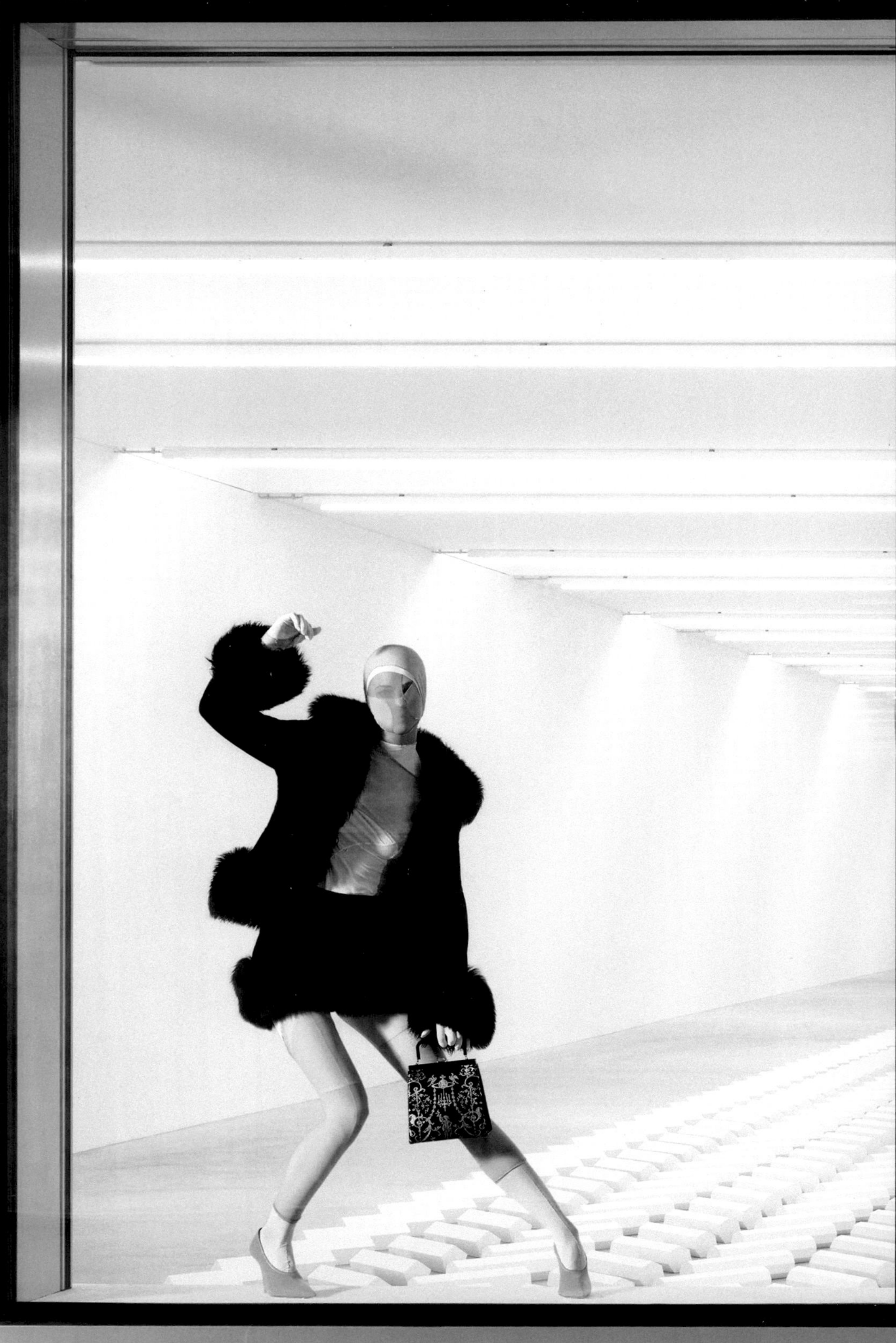

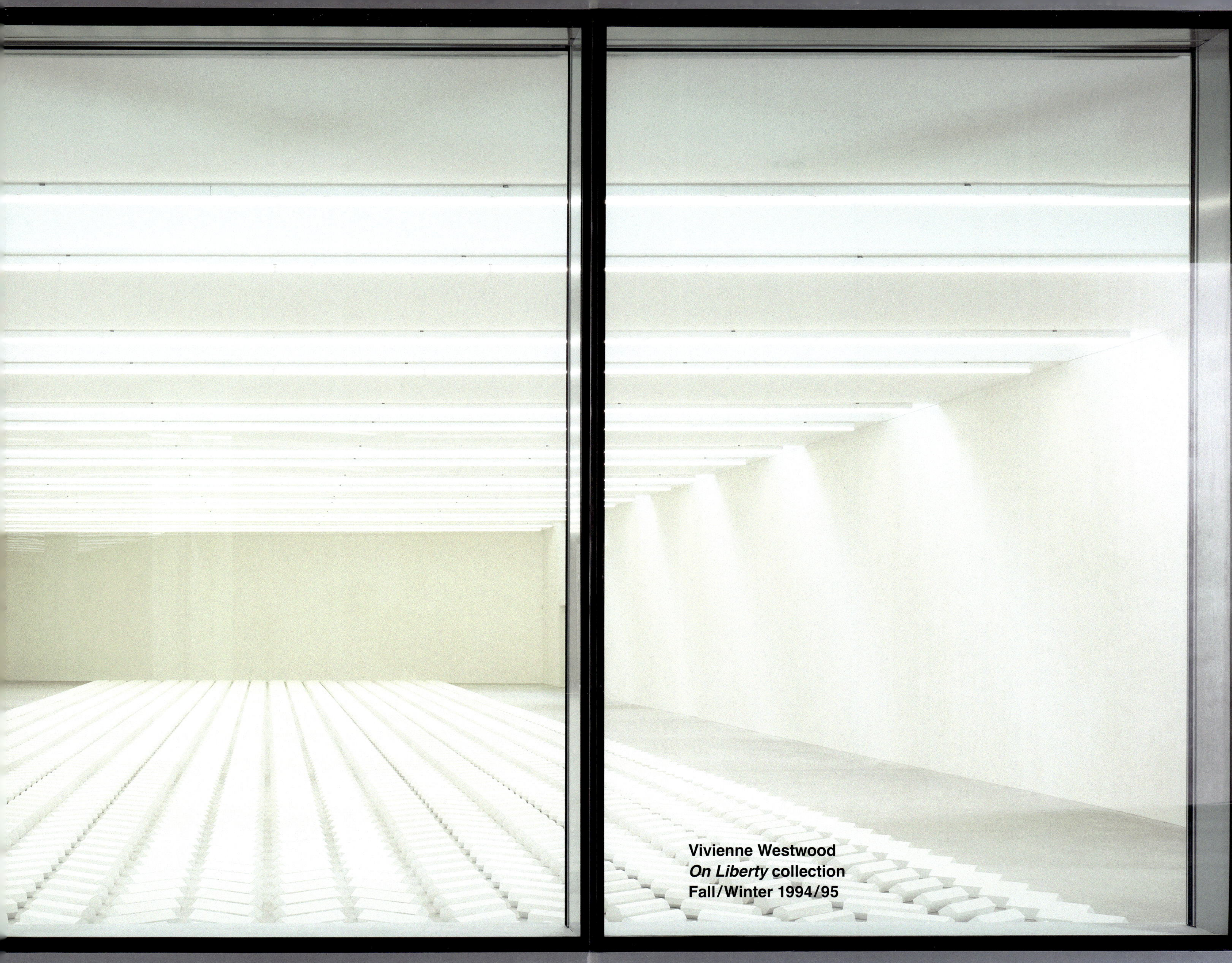

Vivienne Westwood
On Liberty collection
Fall/Winter 1994/95

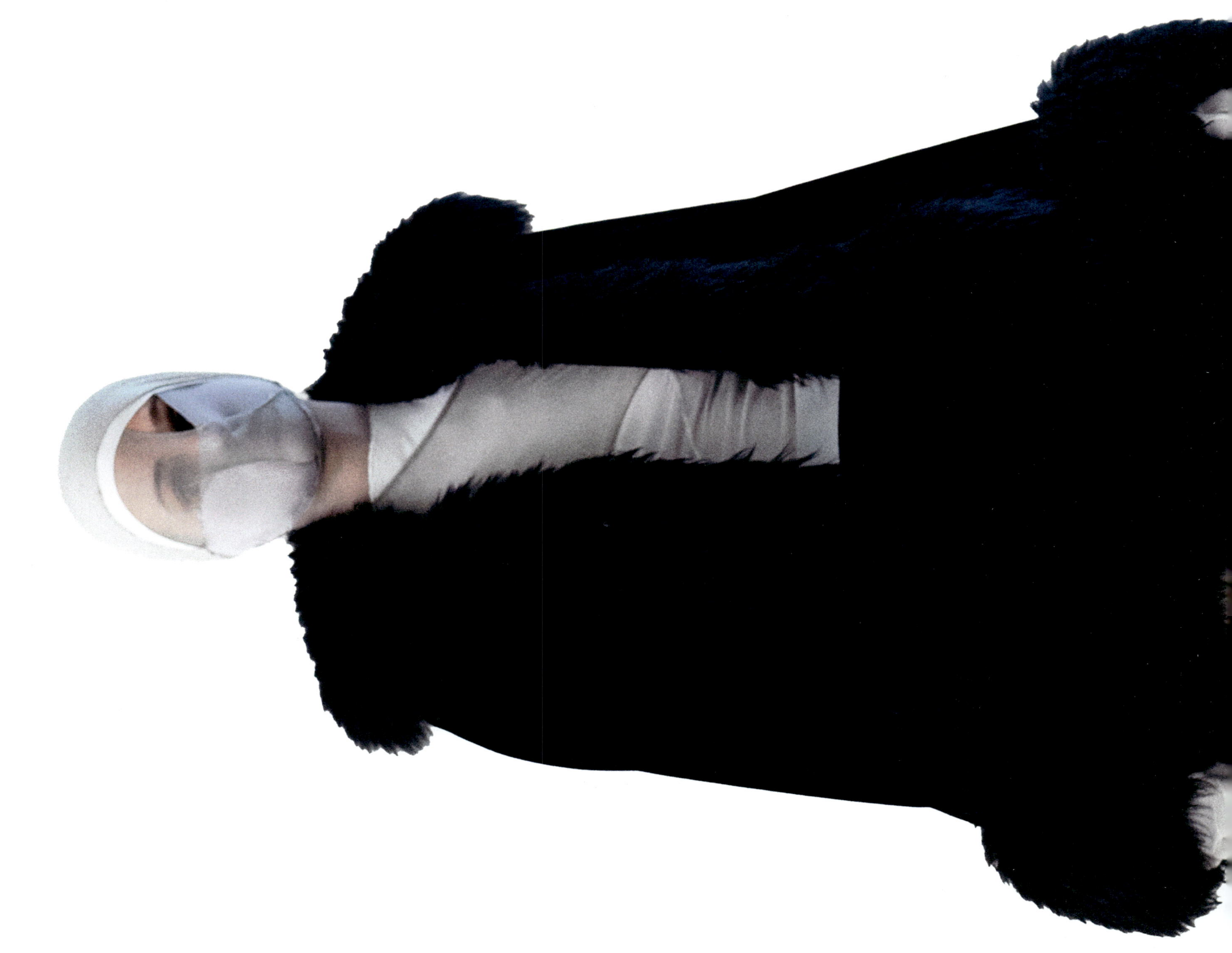

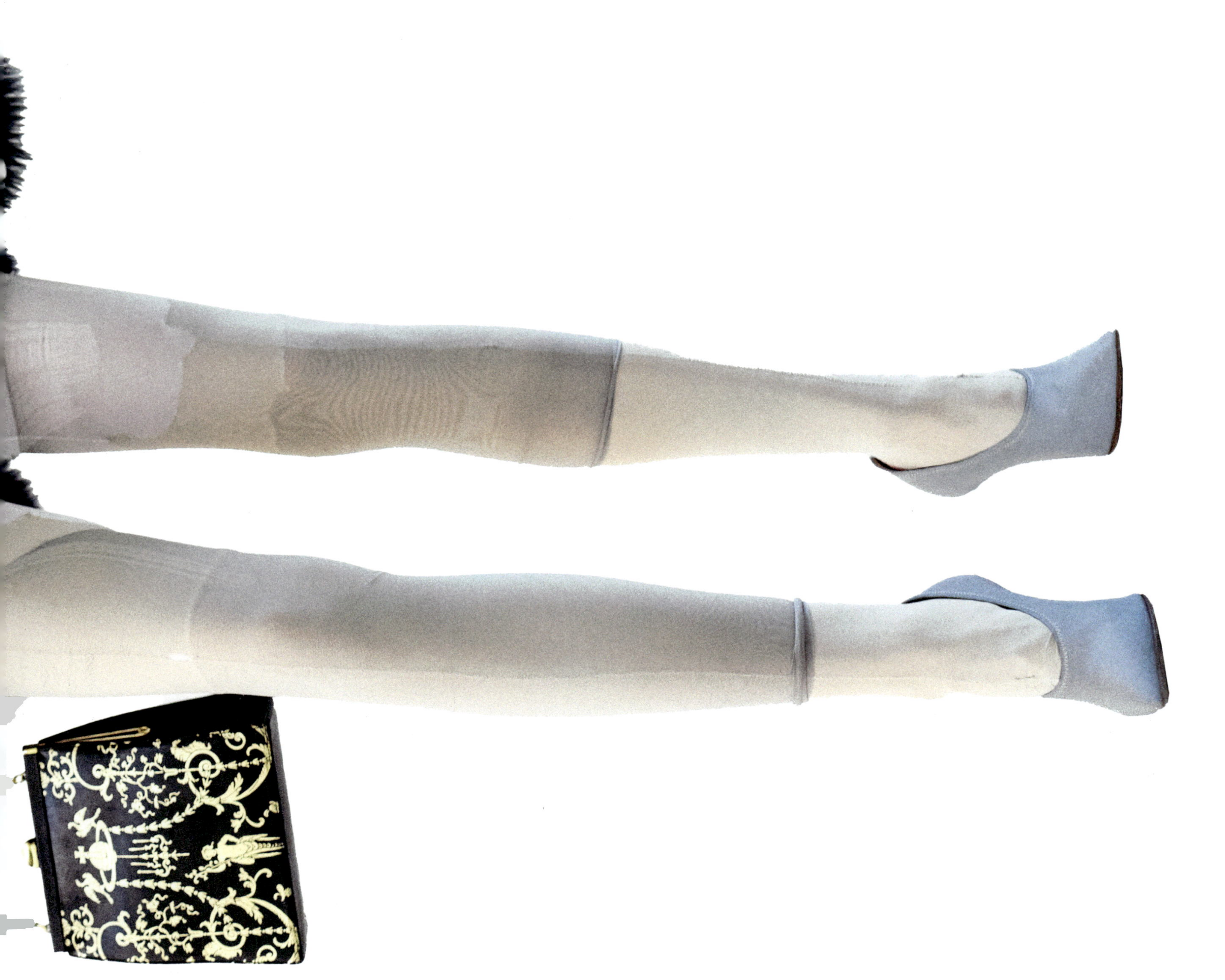

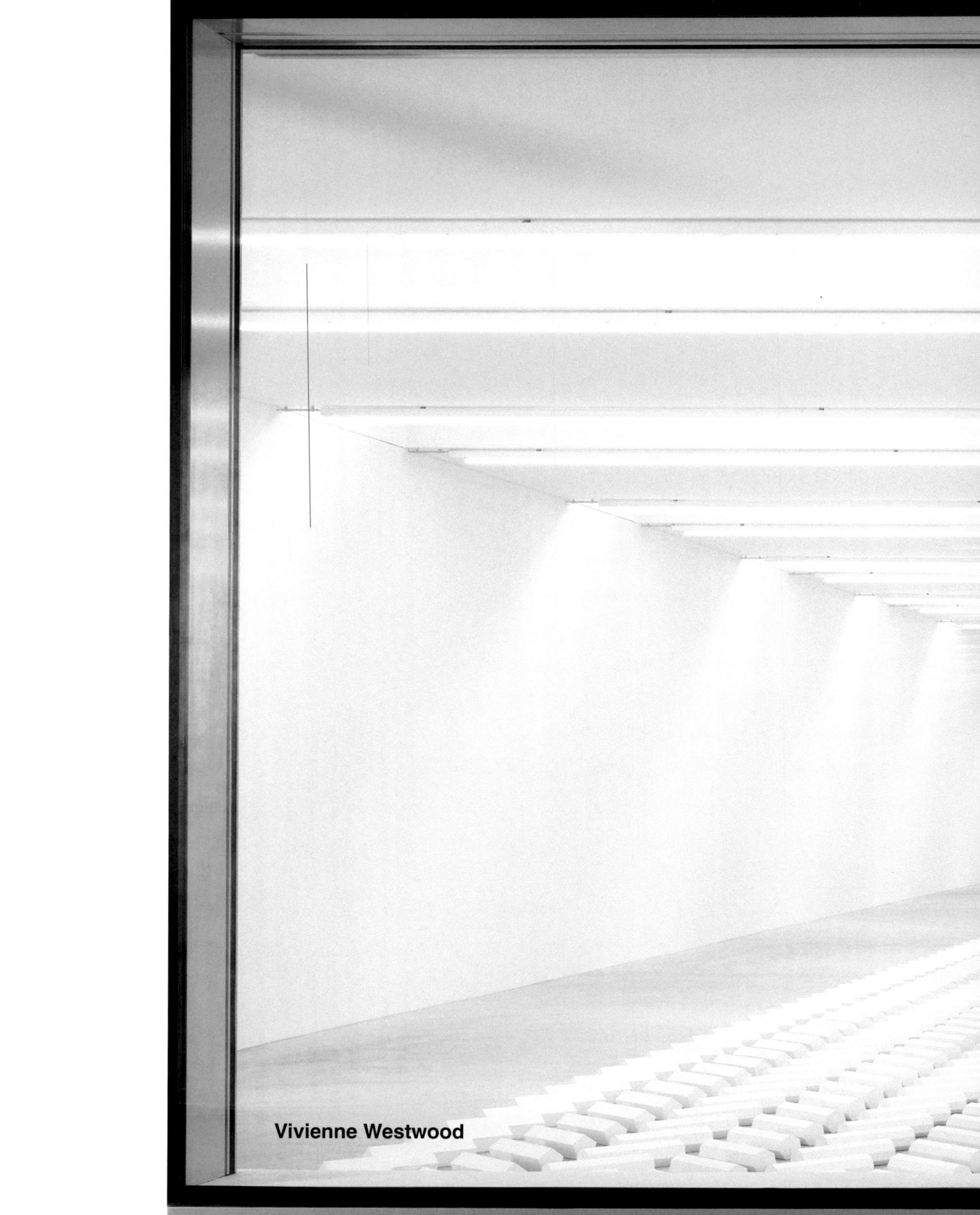
Vivienne Westwood

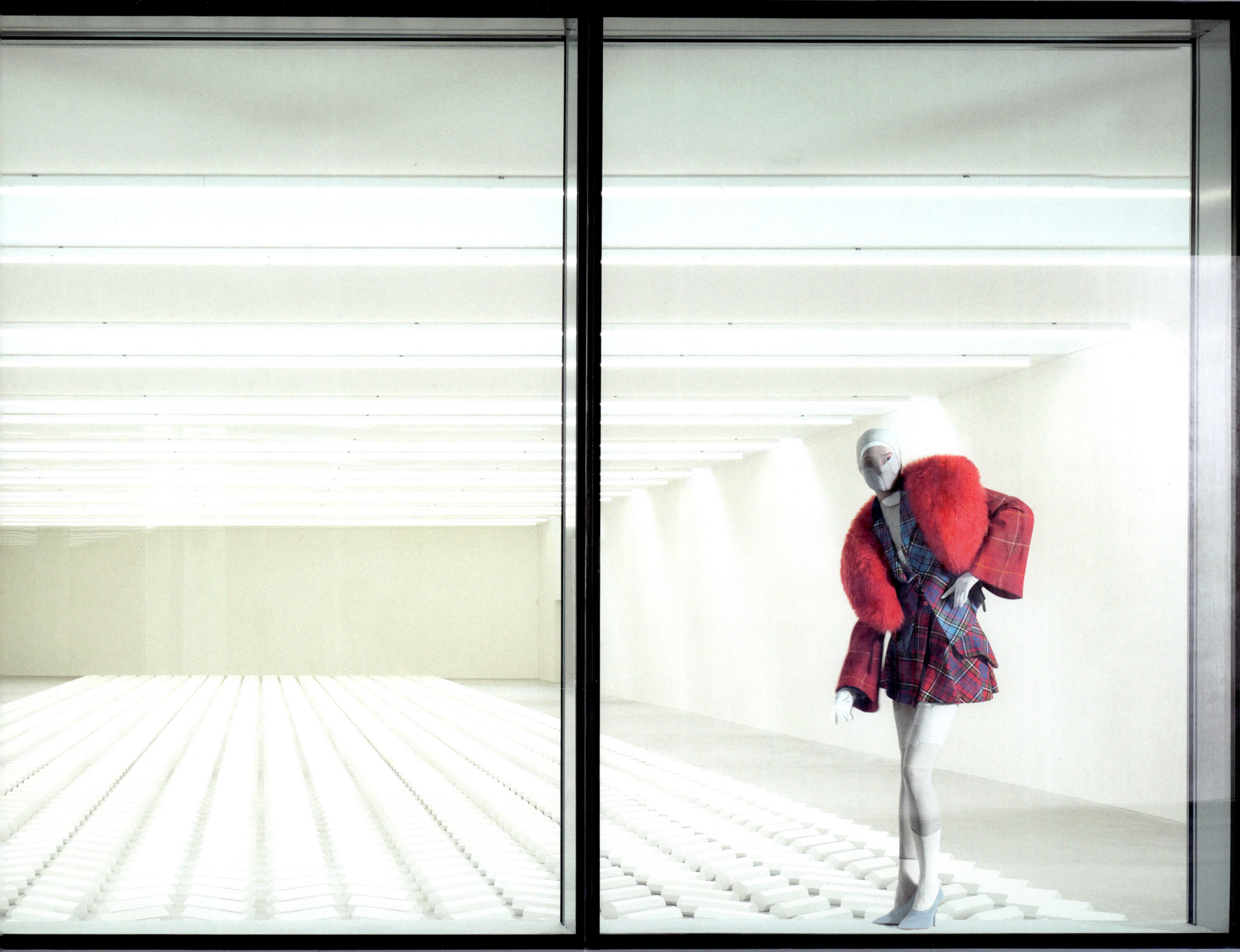

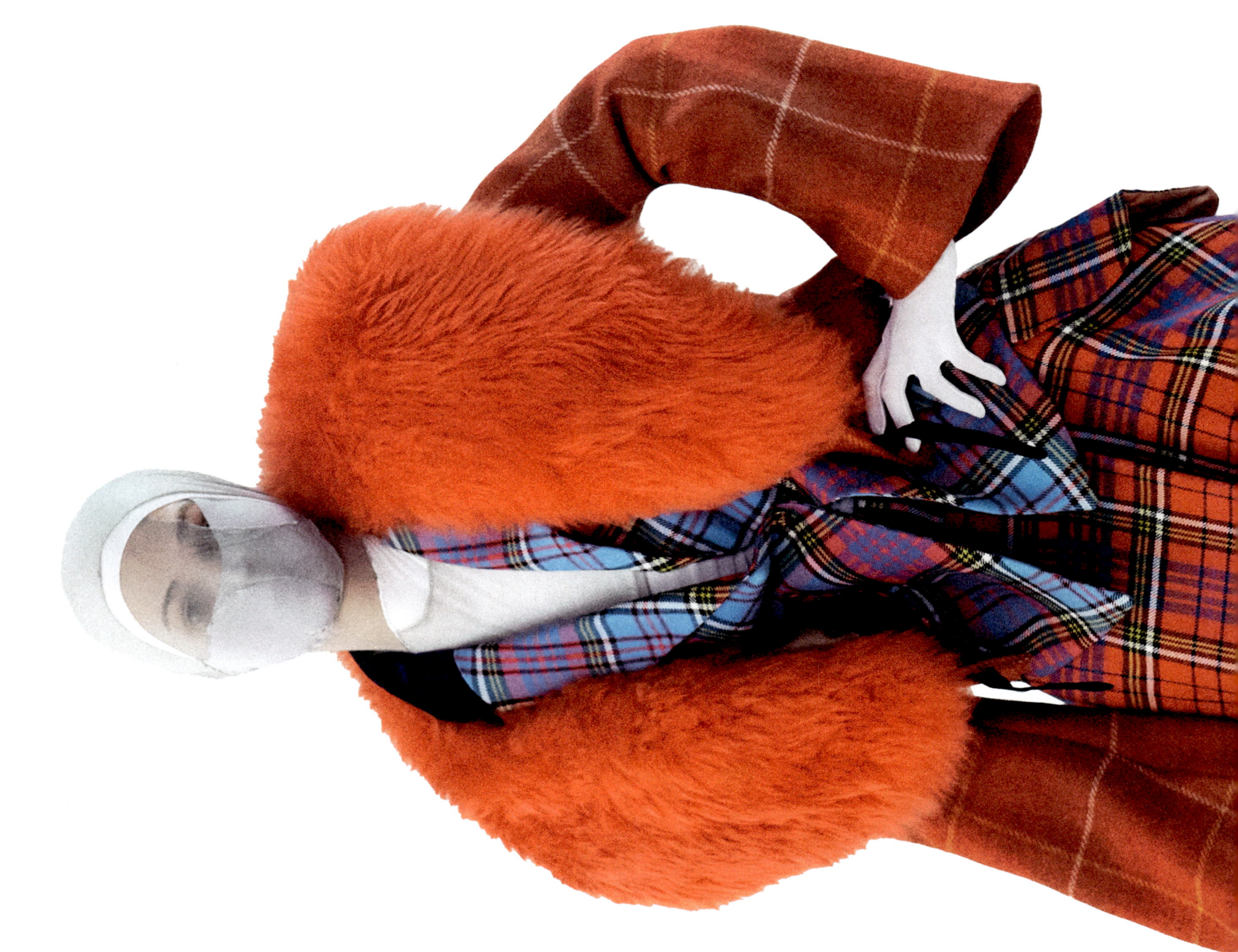

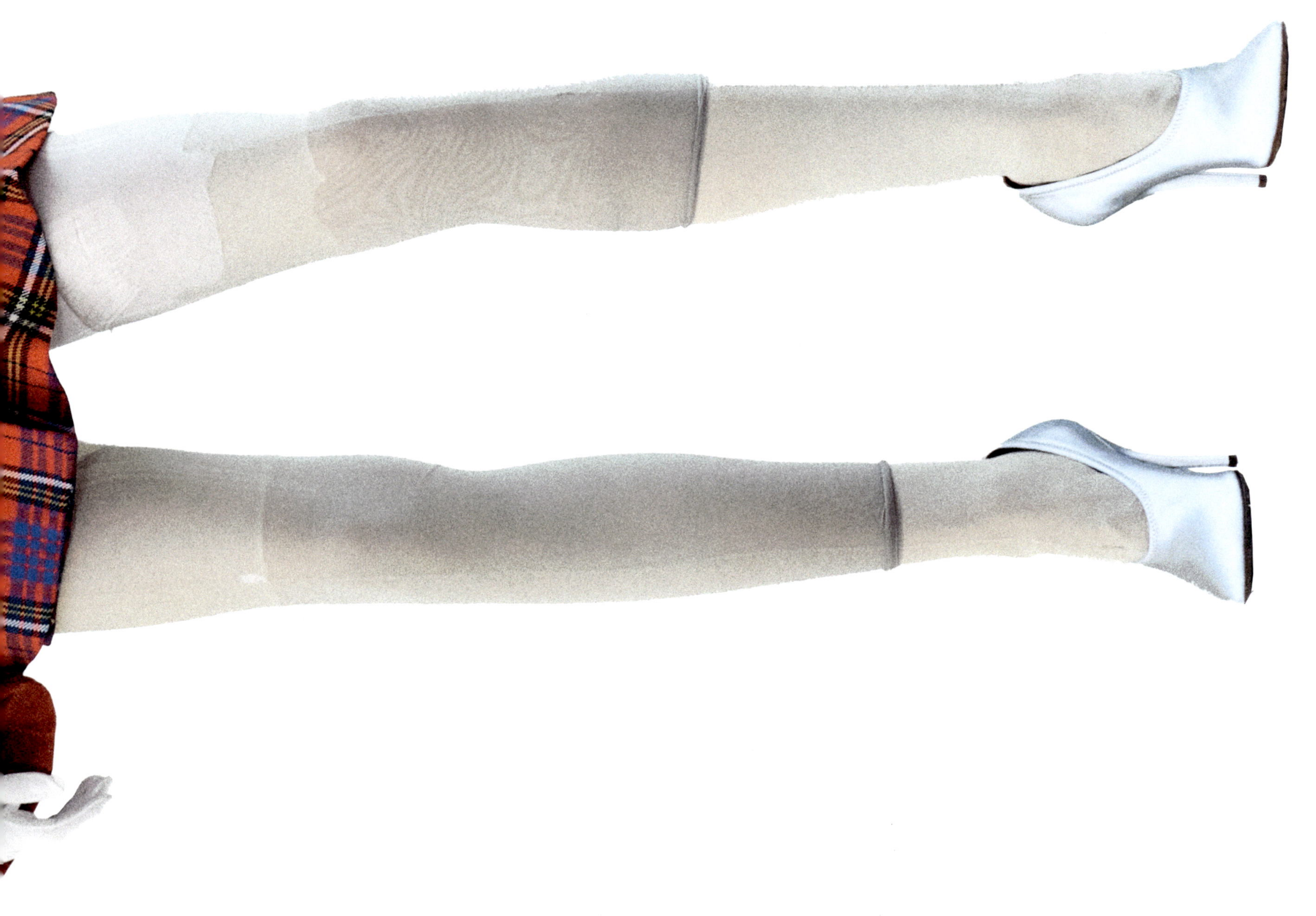

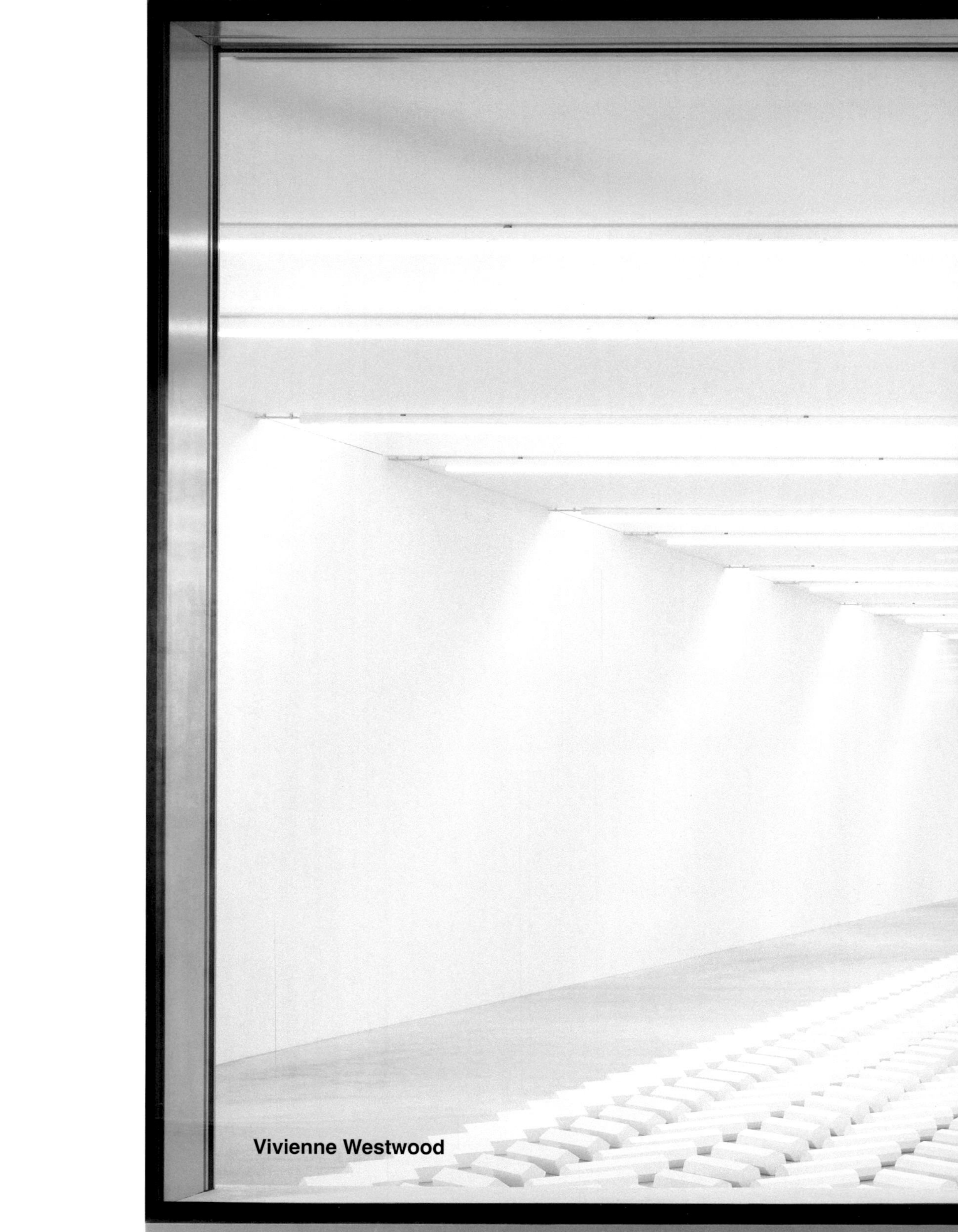
Vivienne Westwood

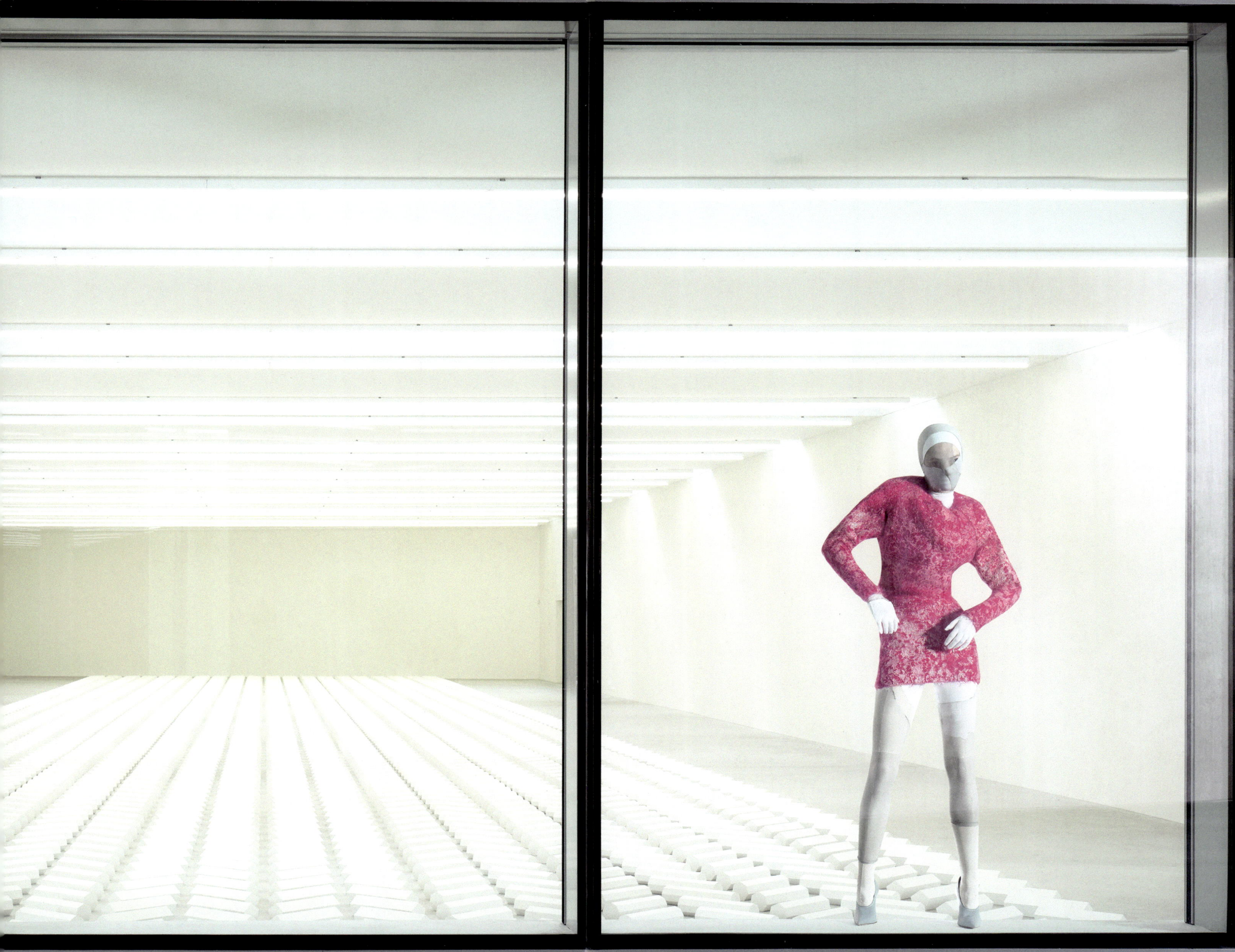

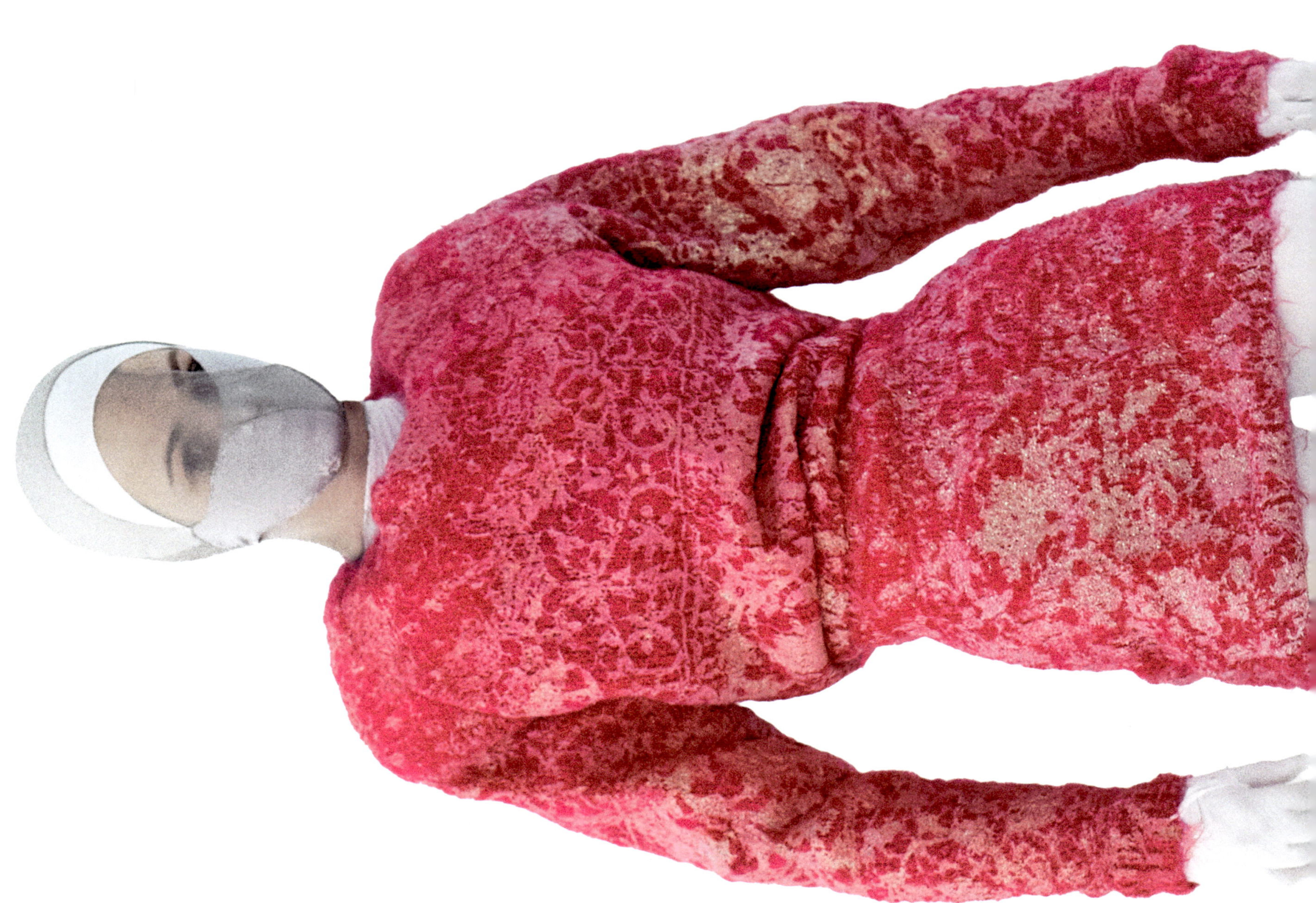

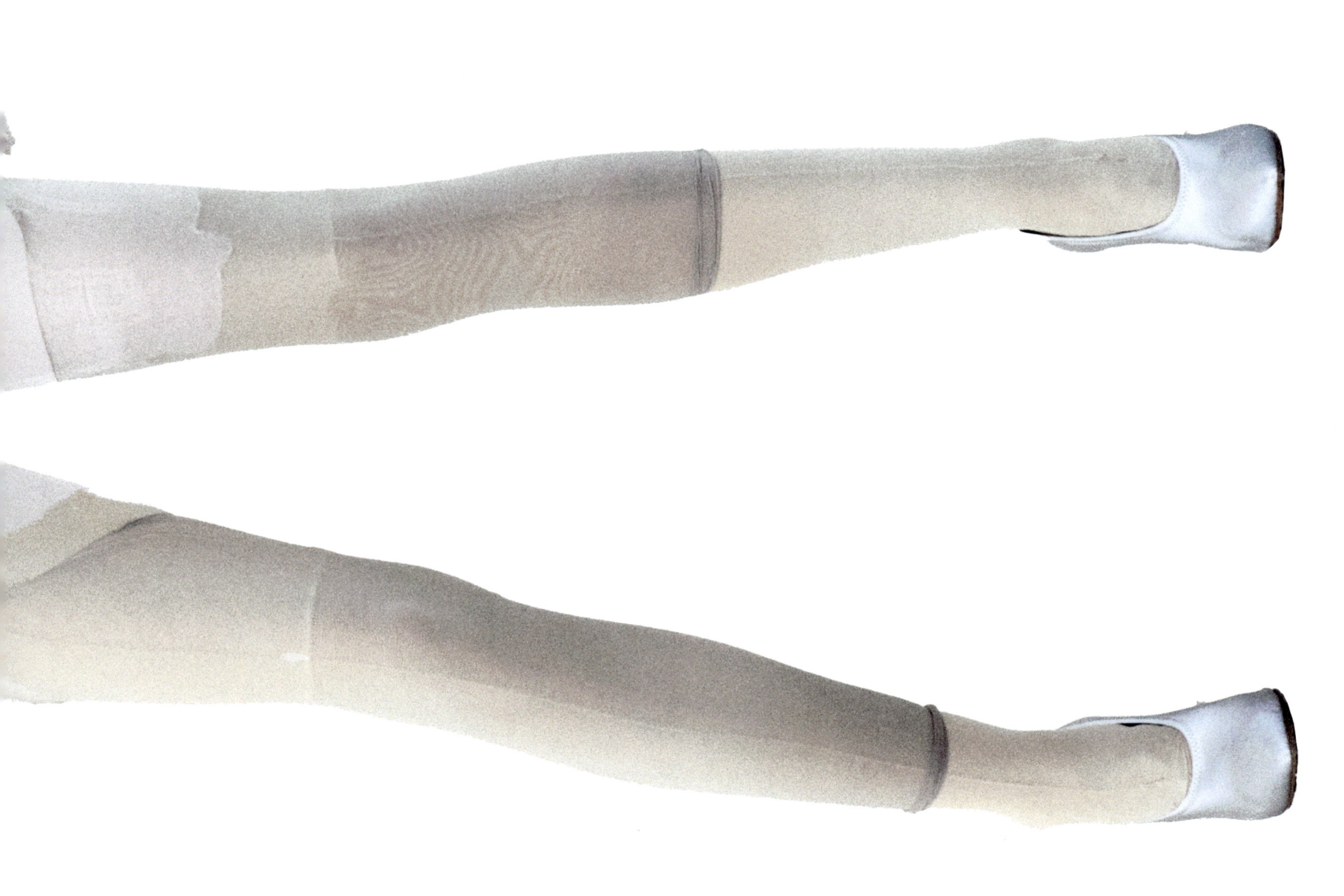

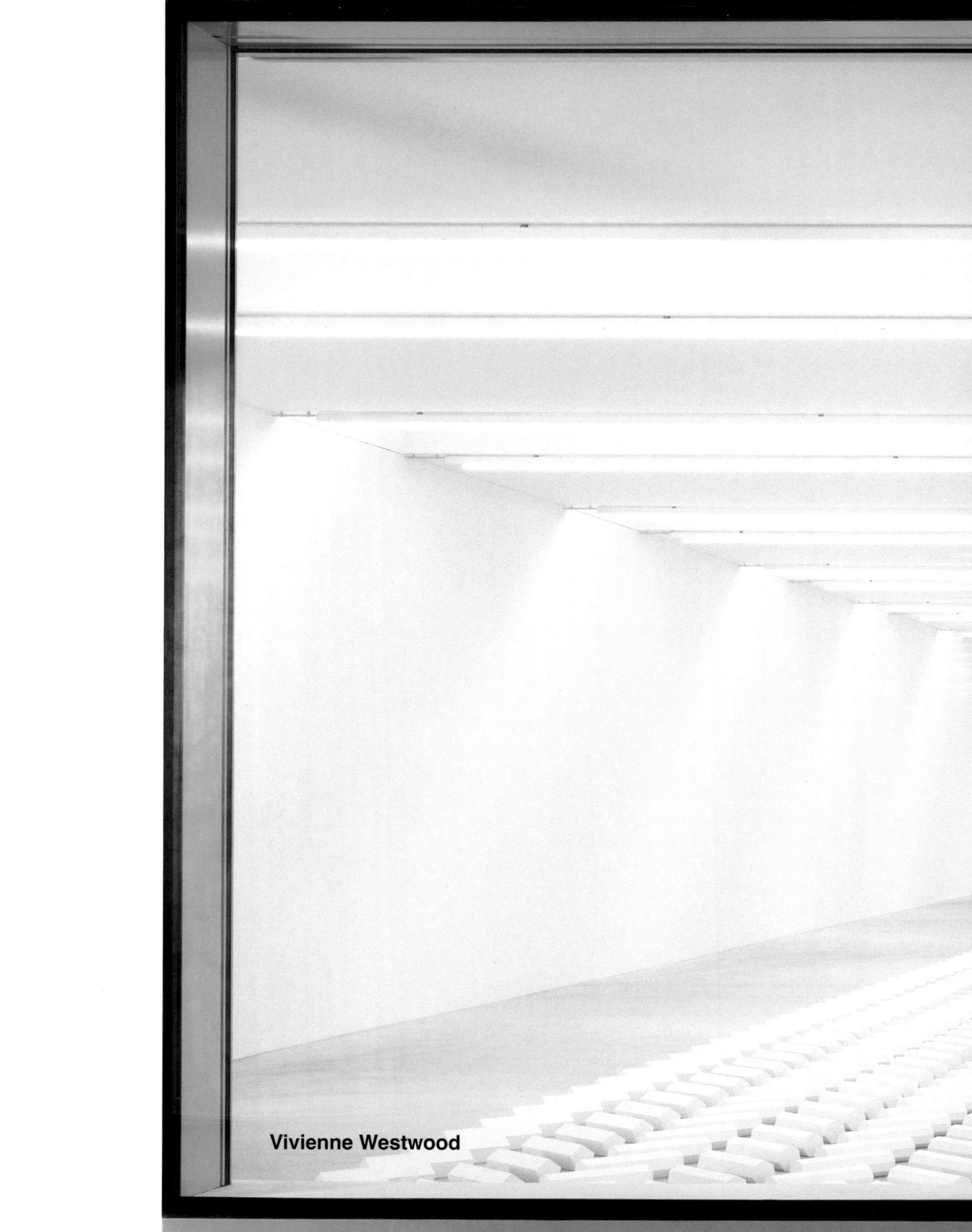
Vivienne Westwood

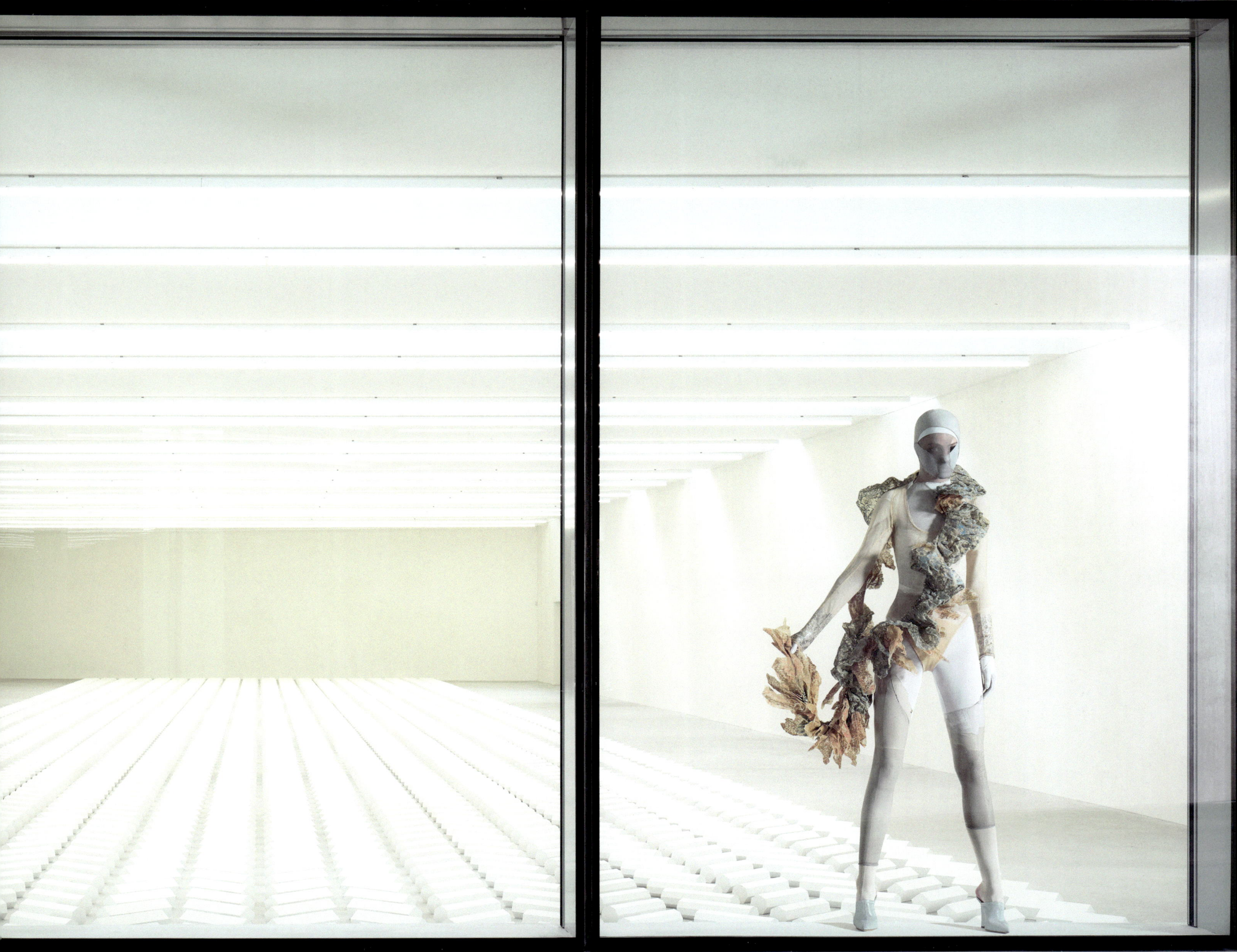

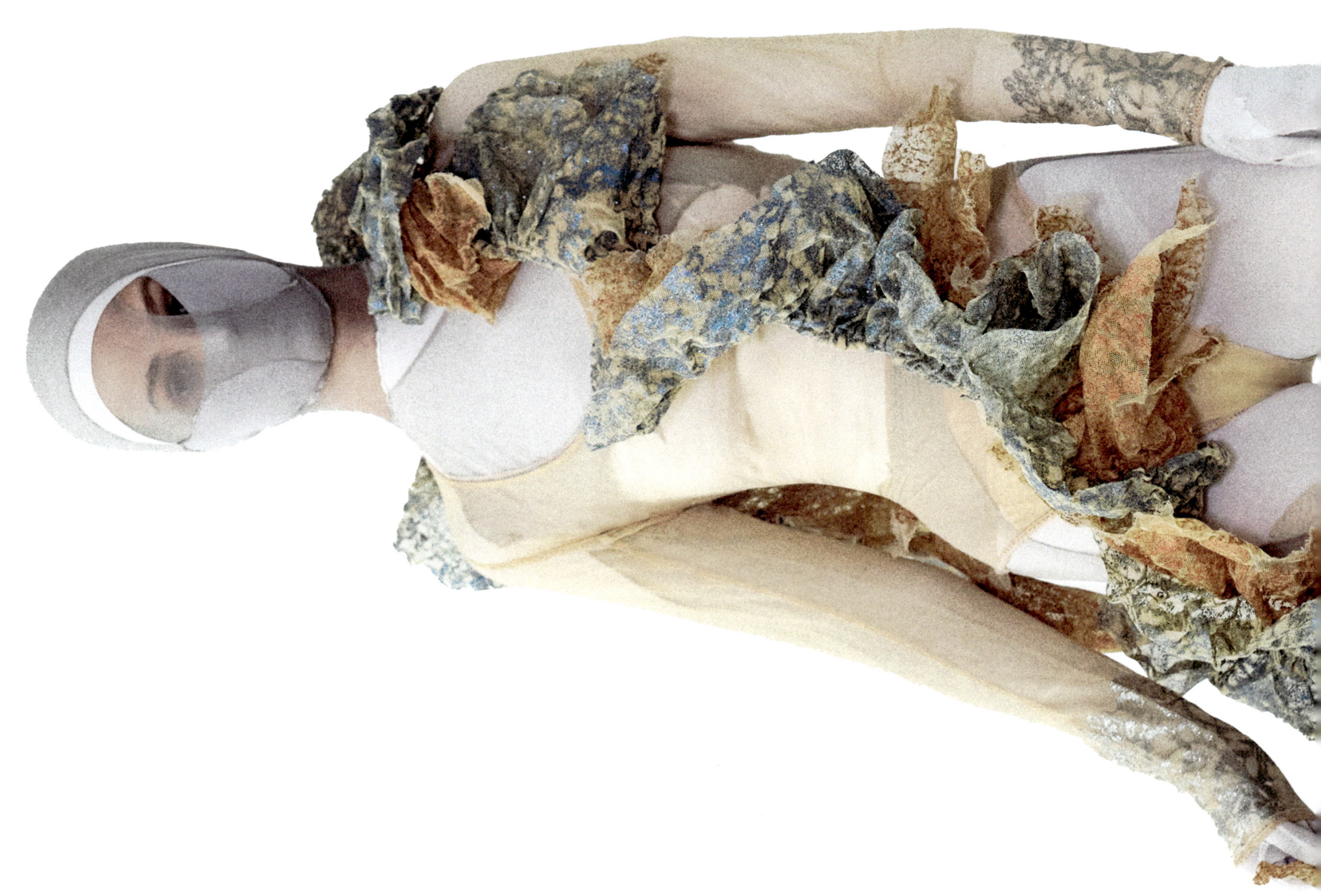

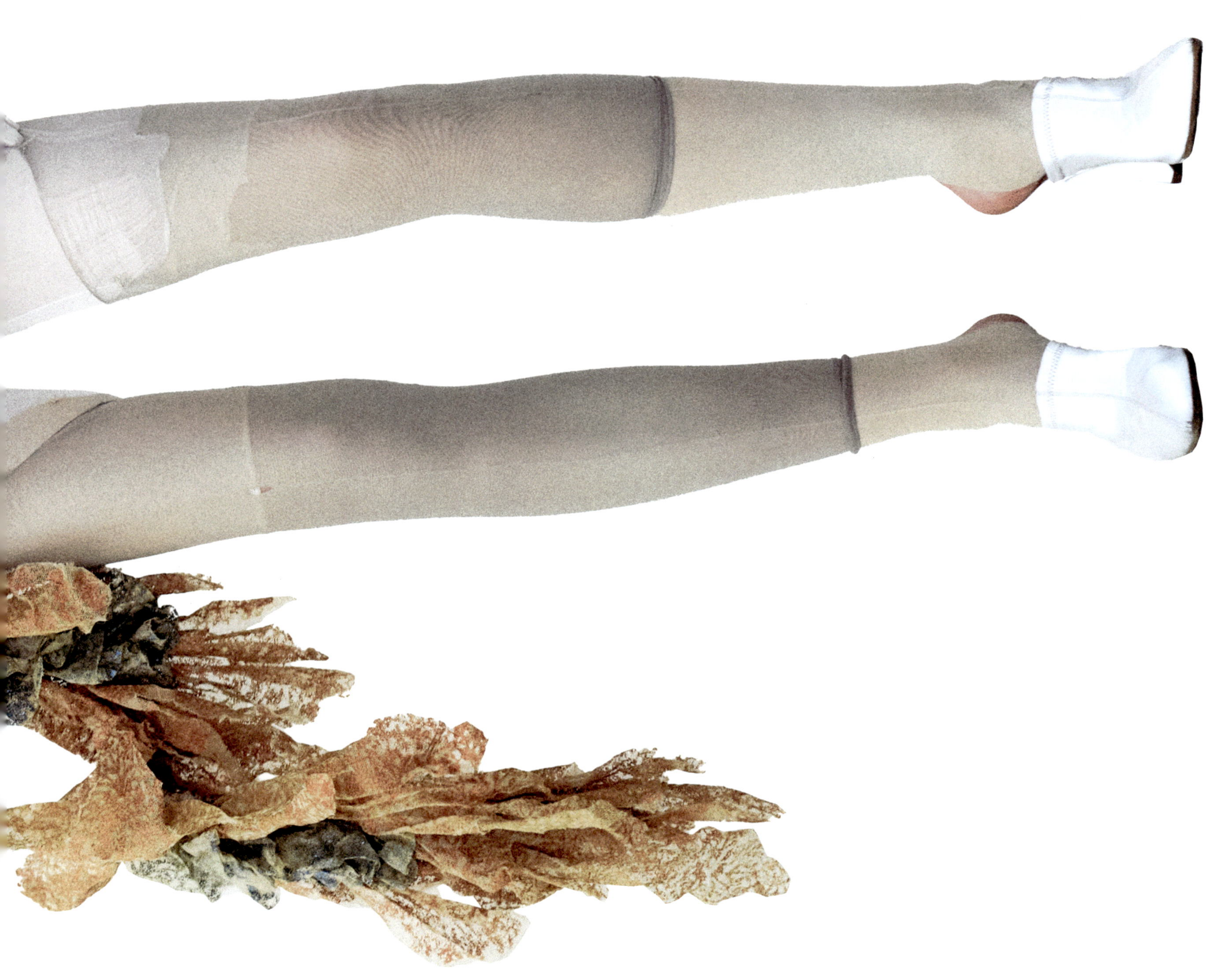

John Galliano
Spring/Summer 1993

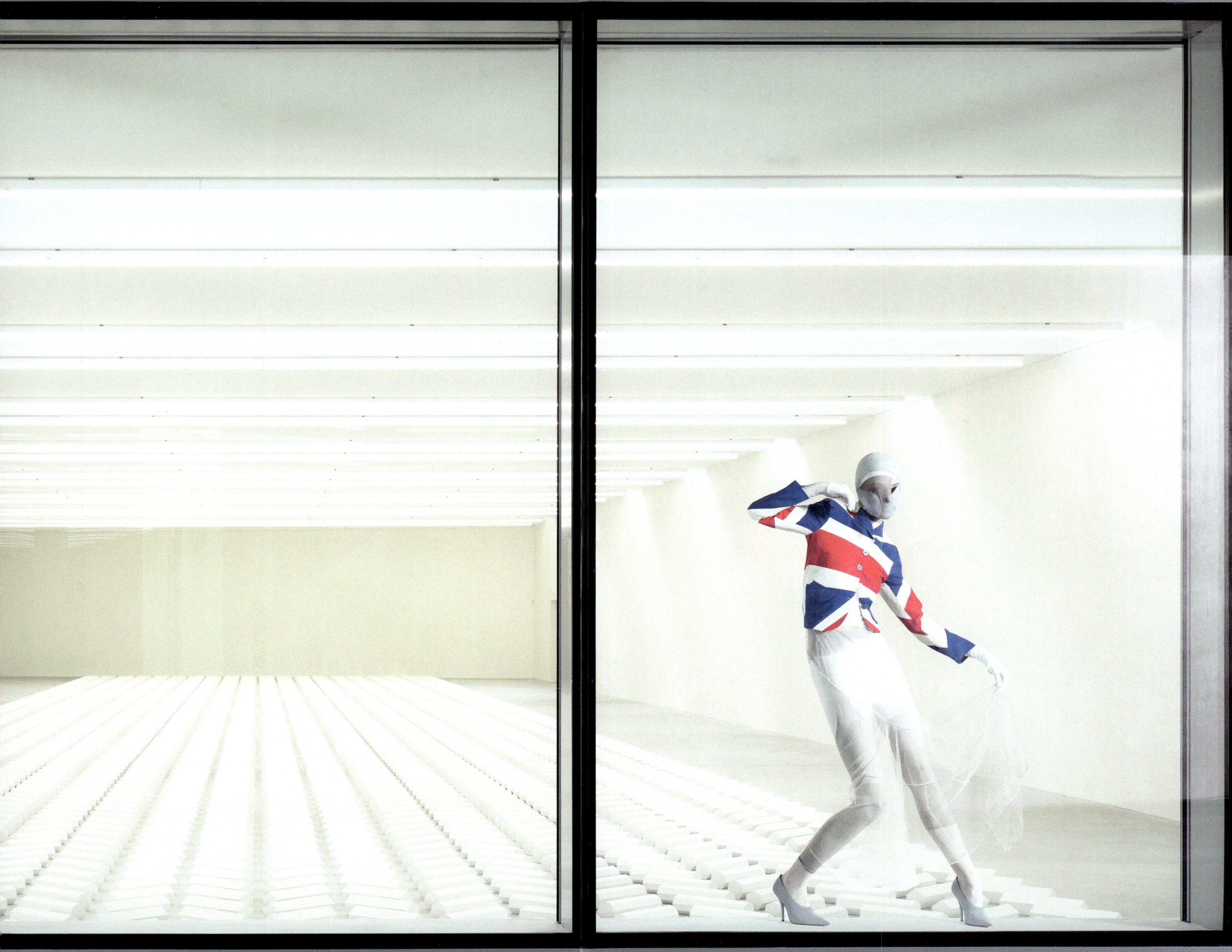

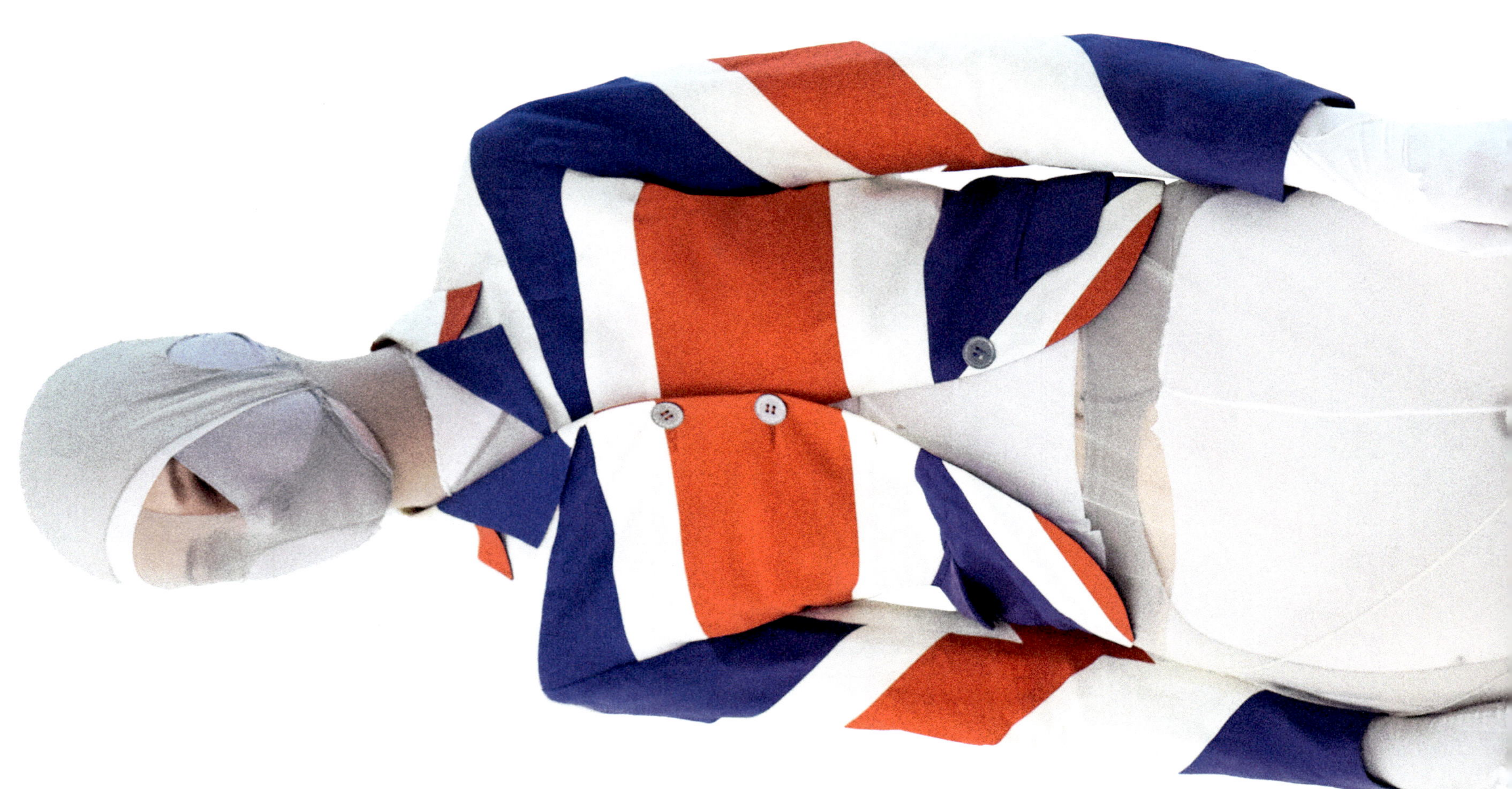

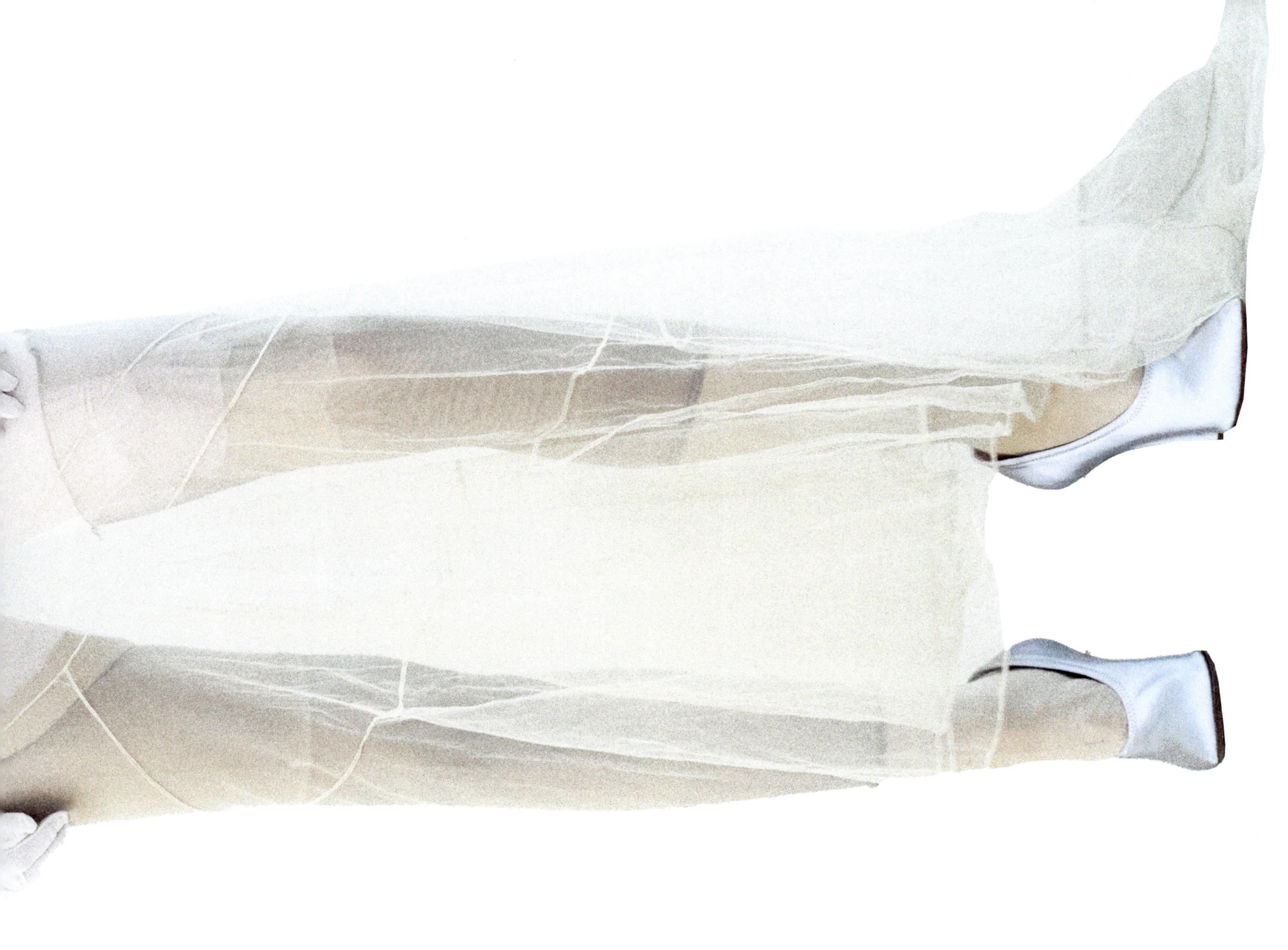

Launched in 1993, Miu Miu, a childhood nickname of Miuccia Prada, the label's designer, was established as the younger alternative to the family's luxury label. Froufrou pieces and shorter cuts defined the brand. This emerald green sleeveless dress from Spring/Summer 1998 reinterprets the mod mini for an uptown appeal. It features a half-skirt overlay with a waisted sash tie, appearing like a deconstructed apron. The collection campaign, shot by Glen Luchford, evoked a tastefully dimmed bordello starring a nubile Zora Starr. A kittenish kink for beau monde daughters. ML

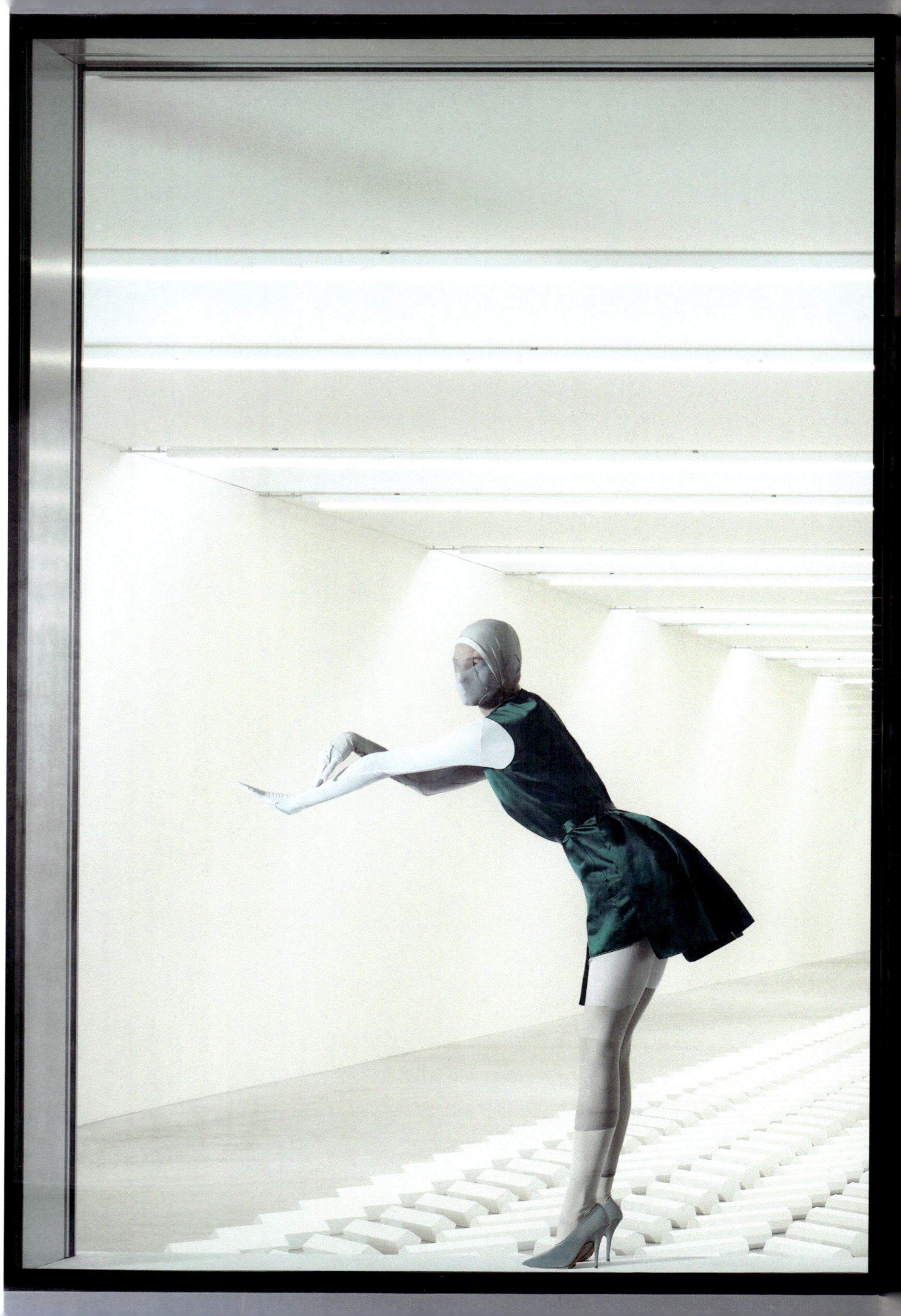

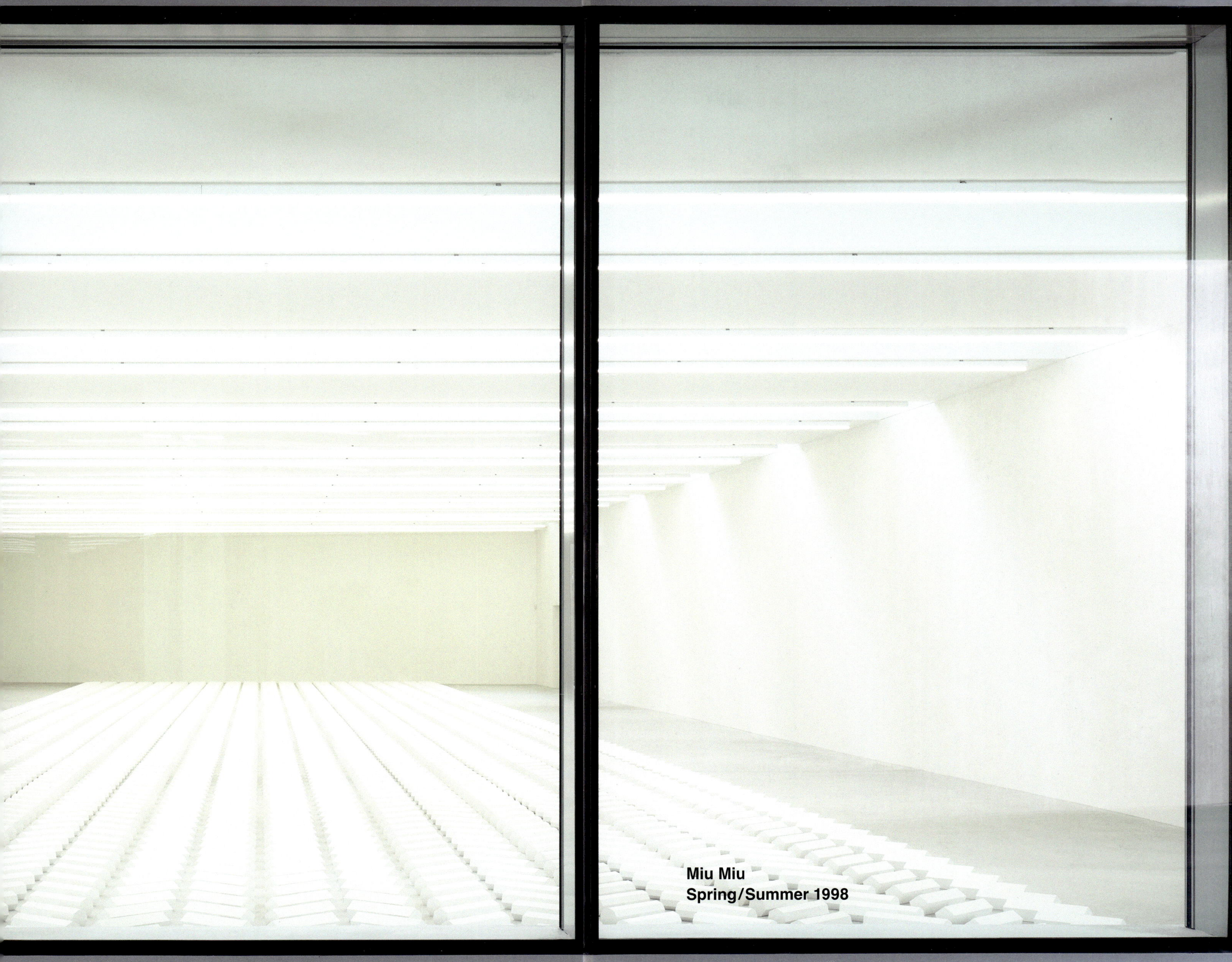
Miu Miu
Spring/Summer 1998

Jean Paul Gaultier
Western Baroque **collection**
Spring/Summer 1989

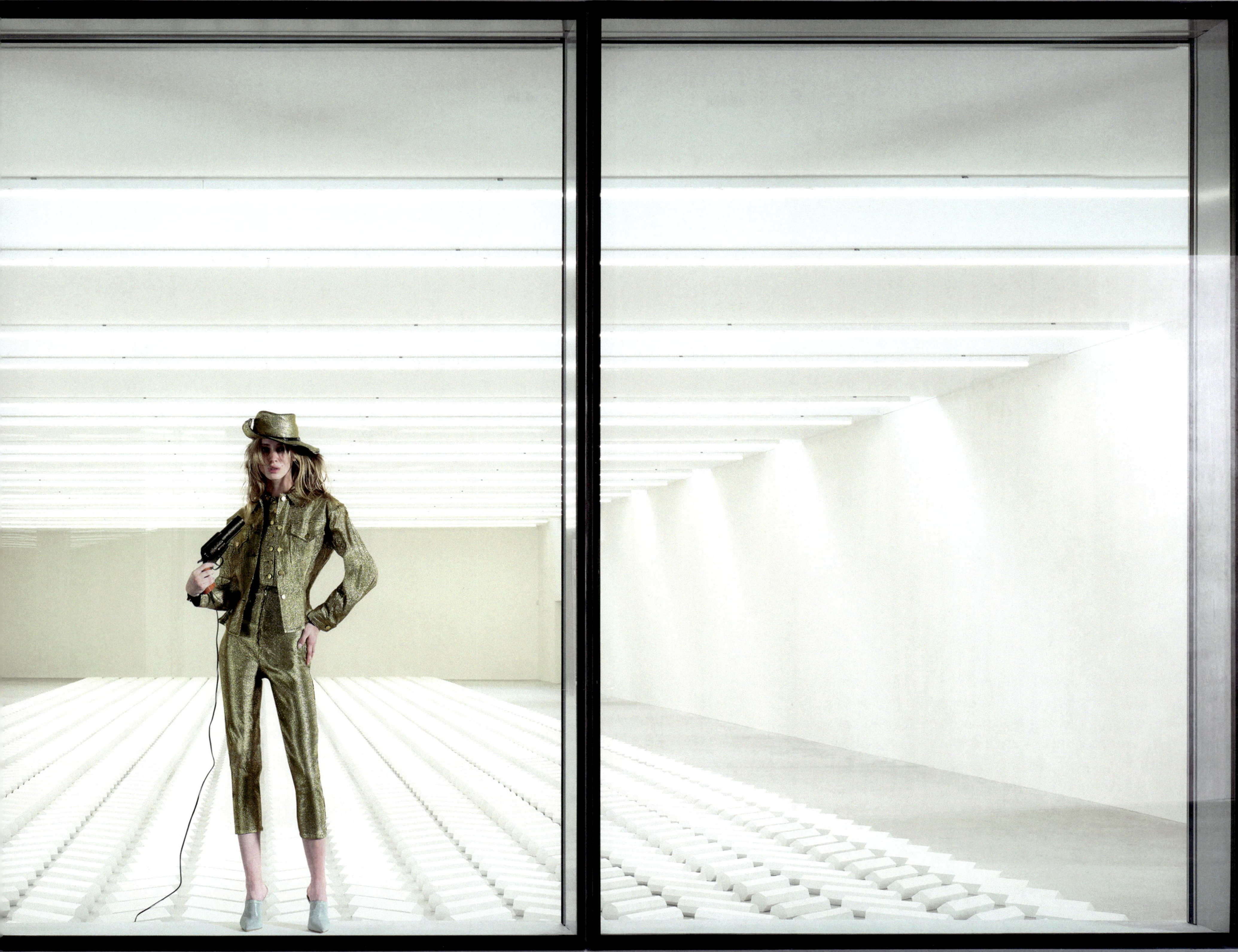

Thierry Mugler's Fall/Winter 1989/90 collection *Hiver Buick* exemplifies the designer's machinic hyper-femininity. Commanding hard edge cuts of metal and reflectors, the collection assimilates Dior's 1947 New Look with automobiles of the same period, particularly those designed by Harley J. Earl. This synched-in waisted black jacket features a chrome metal Cadillac grill that accentuates the hip curvature. The aerodynamically angular cuffs are completed by cufflinks in the exaggerated tail shape of a 1959 Cadillac tailfin. A futuristic techno-carapace appeal; mechanophilia propaganda for High Street. ML

Thierry Mugler
Hiver Buick collection
Fall/Winter 1989/90

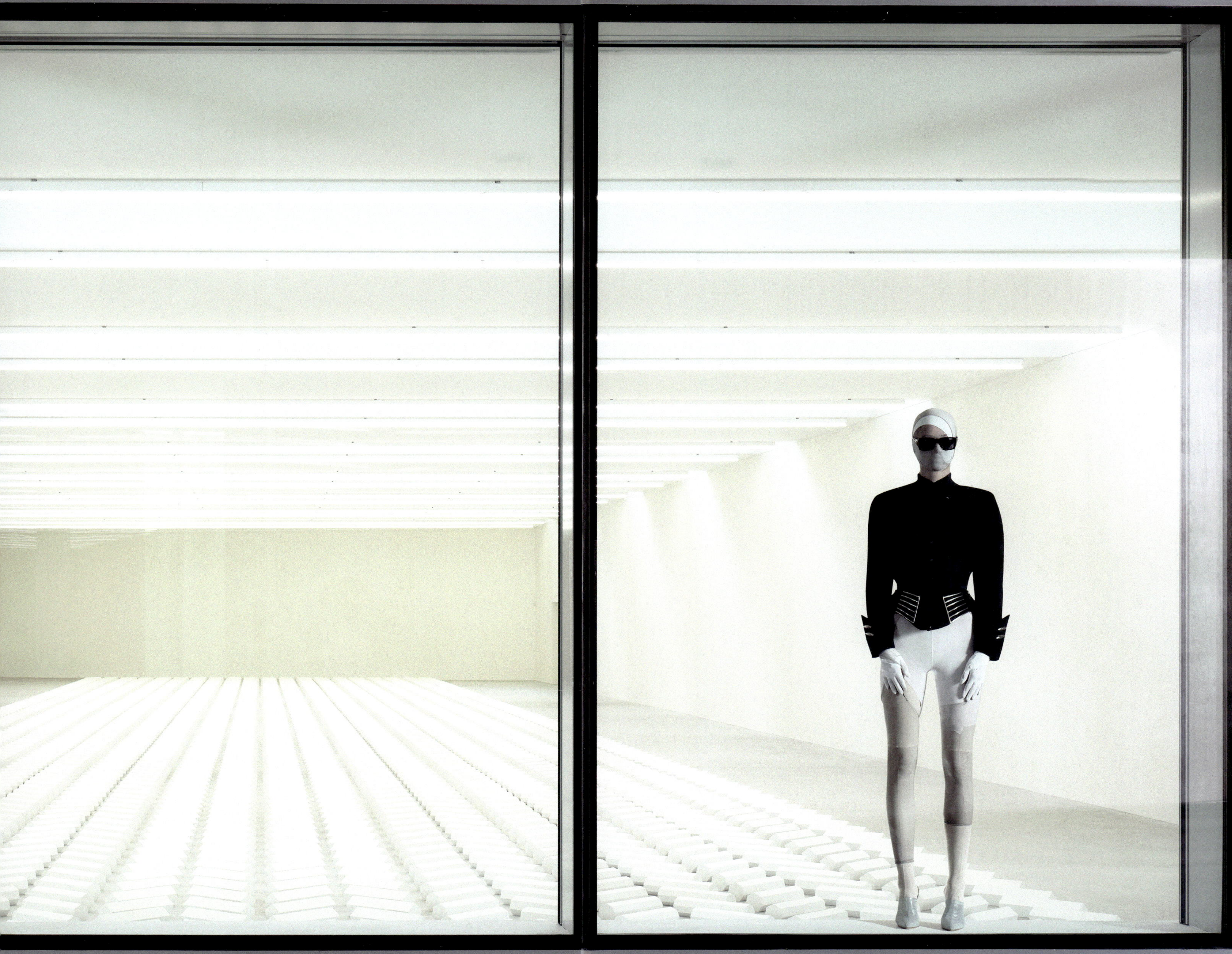

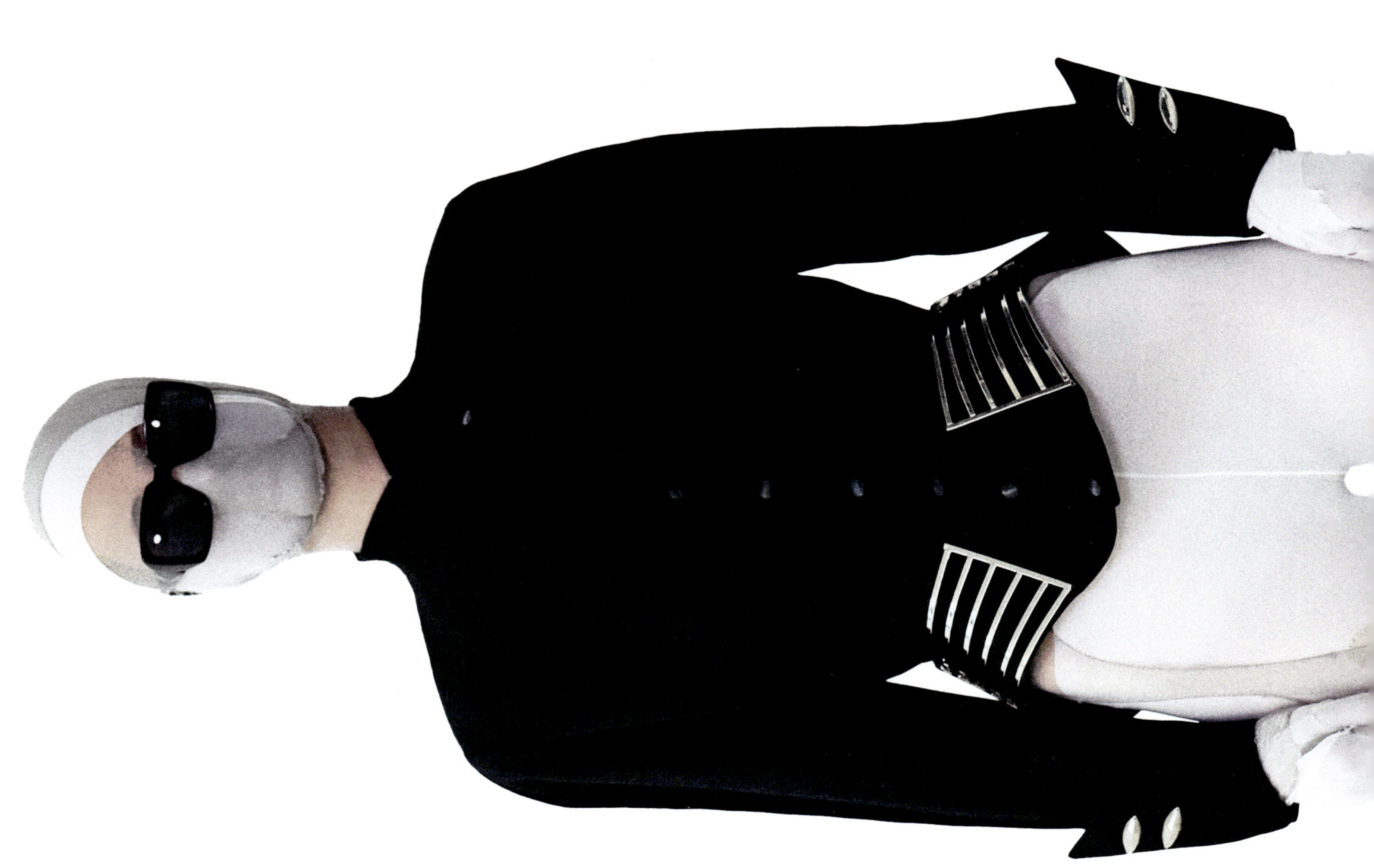

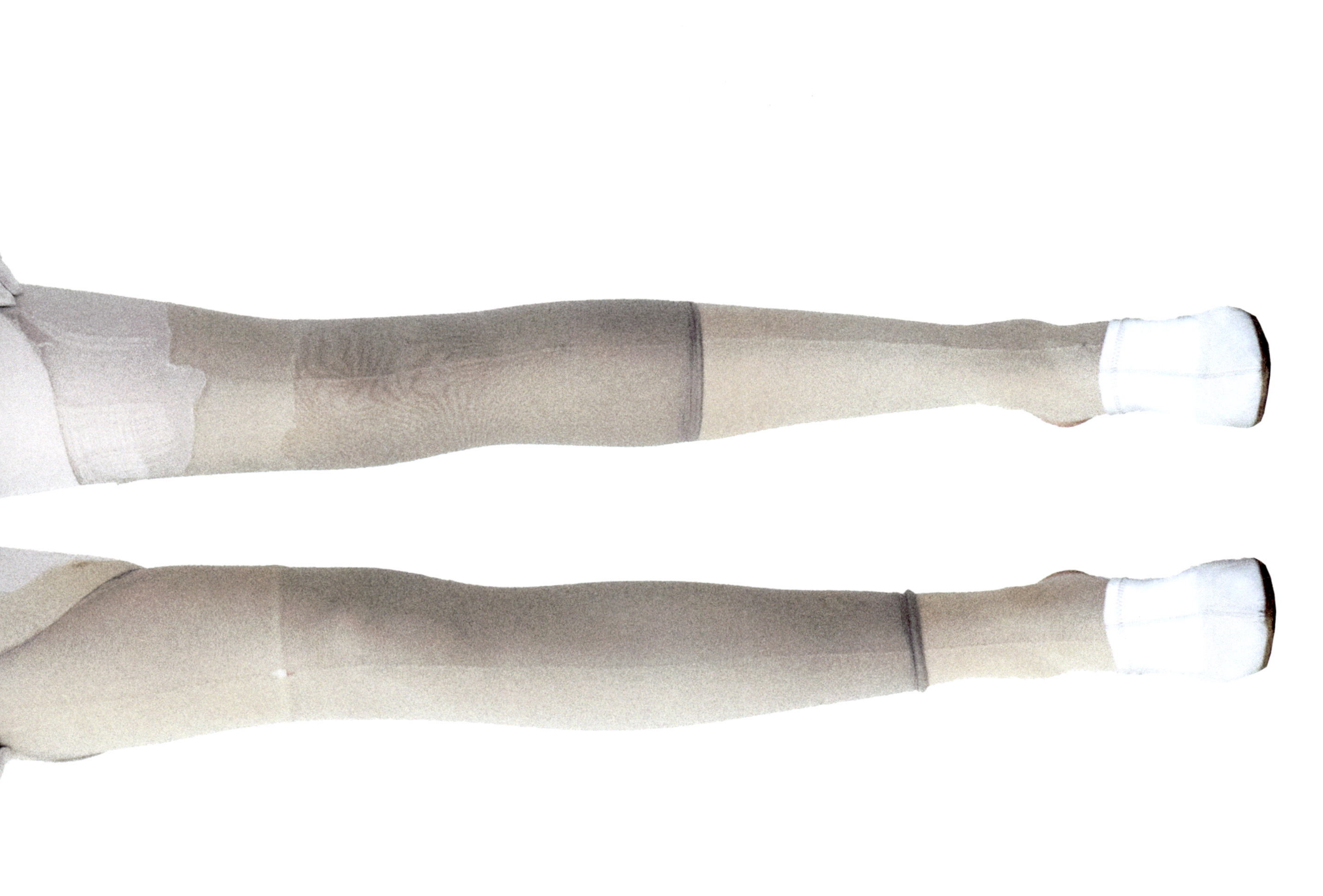

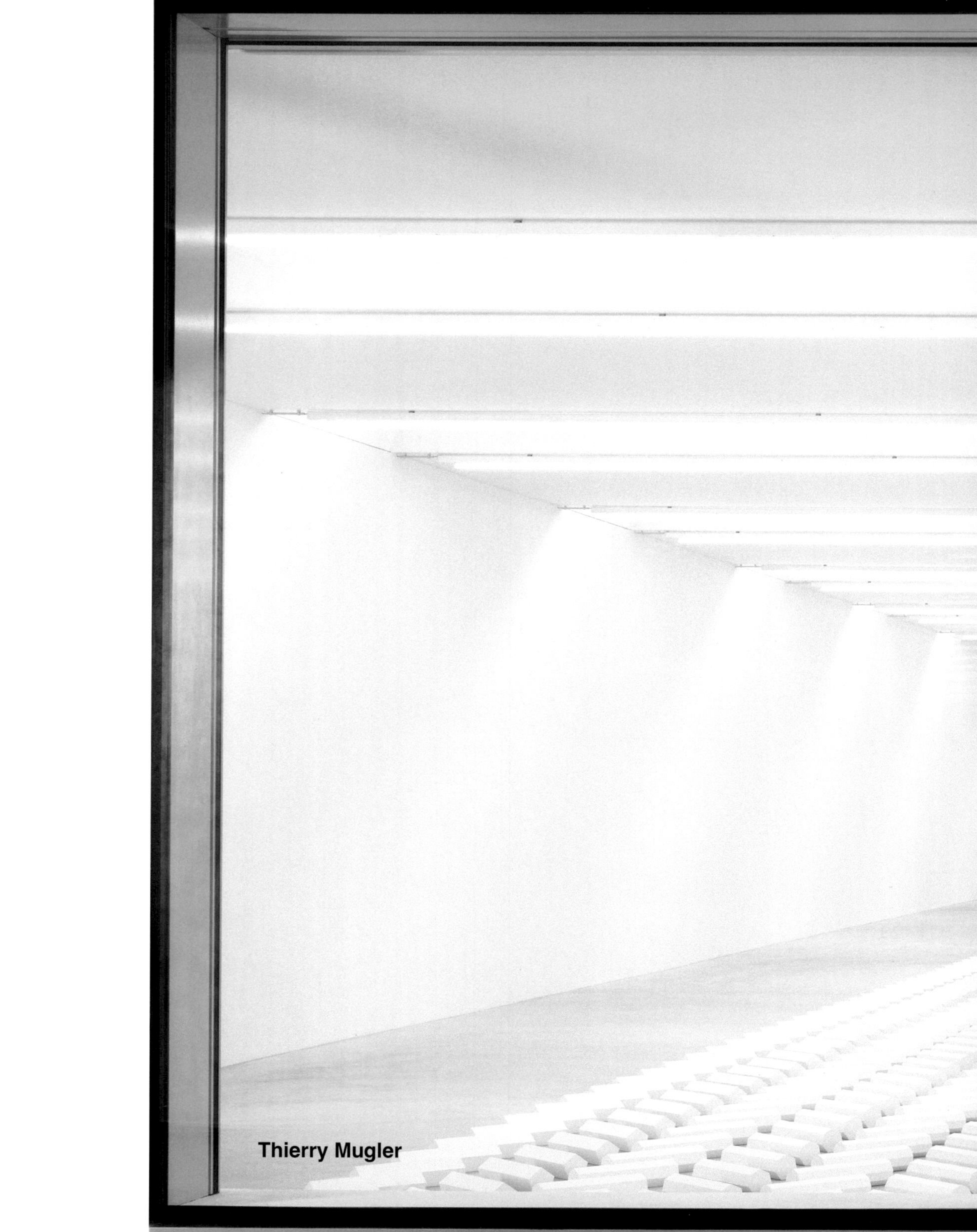
Thierry Mugler

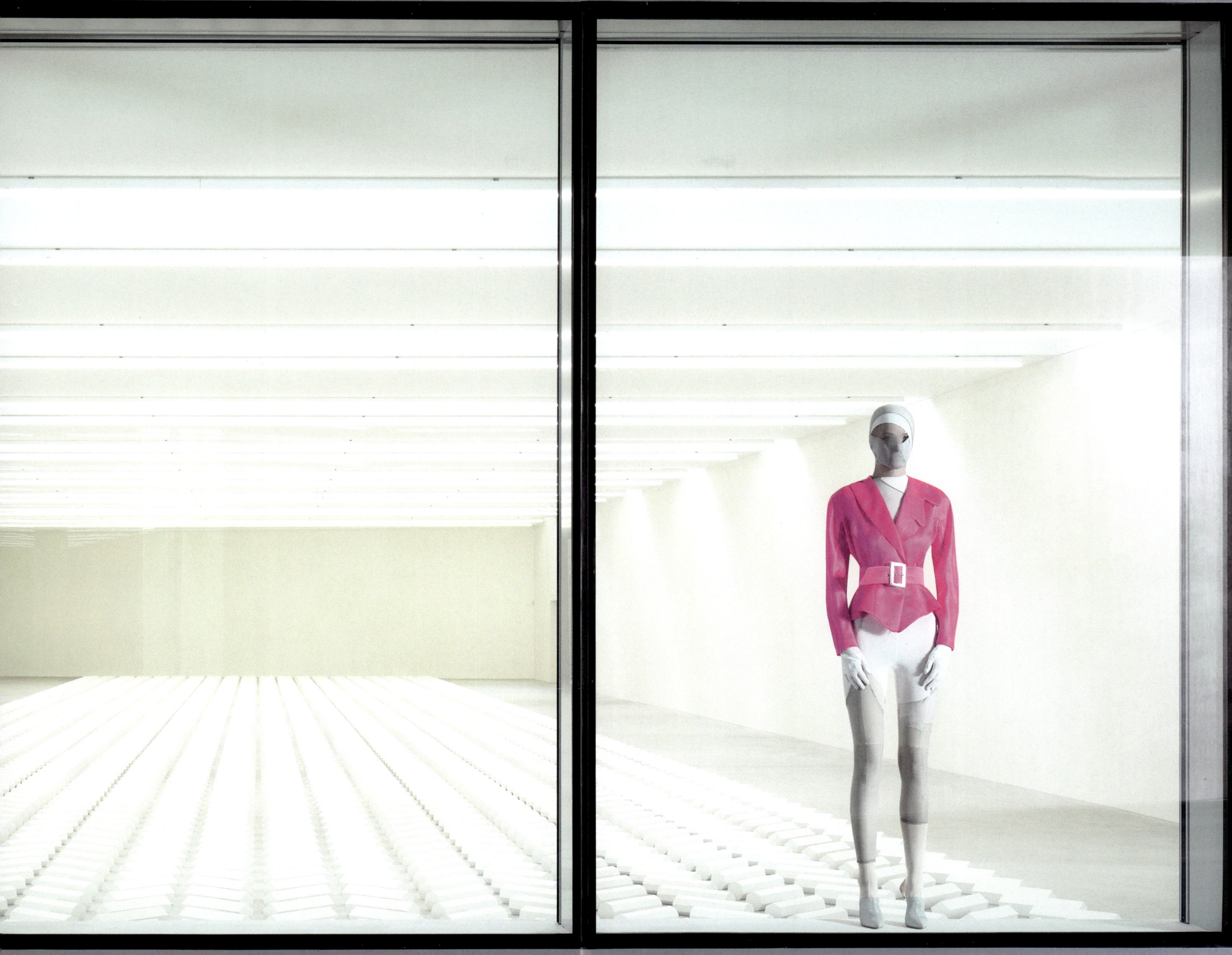

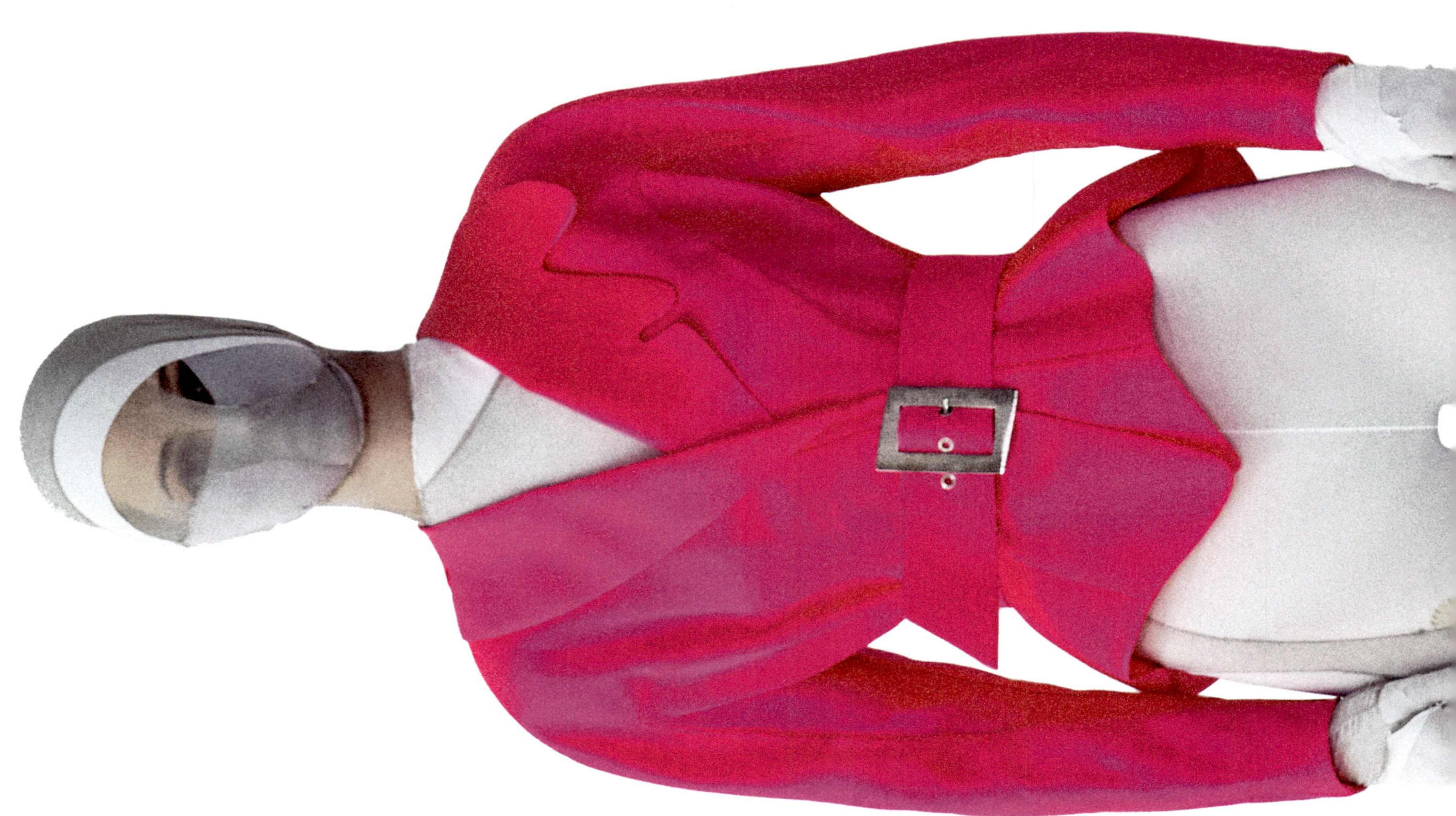

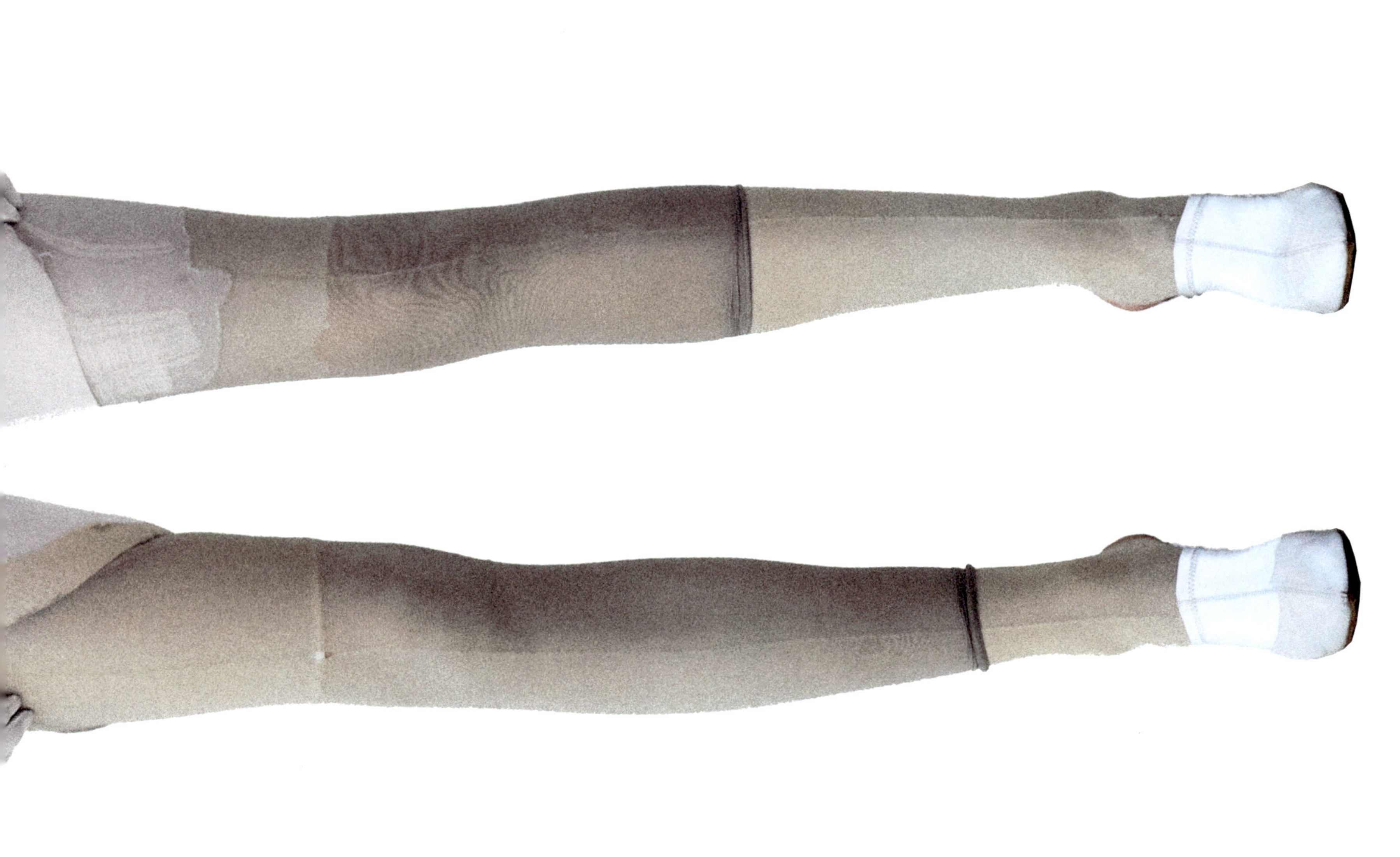

This two-piece suit from Spring/Summer 1990 demonstrates Mugler's piercing graphic imprint through the use of design lines (functionless, aesthetic seams that piece a garment). The waved design lines seen here orbit the body to construct a rainbow-pieced pattern. A retina display colorway of plastic candy, homosexual pride, and acid house. What better constellation of signs to map the zeitgeist? ML

Thierry Mugler
Spring/Summer 1990

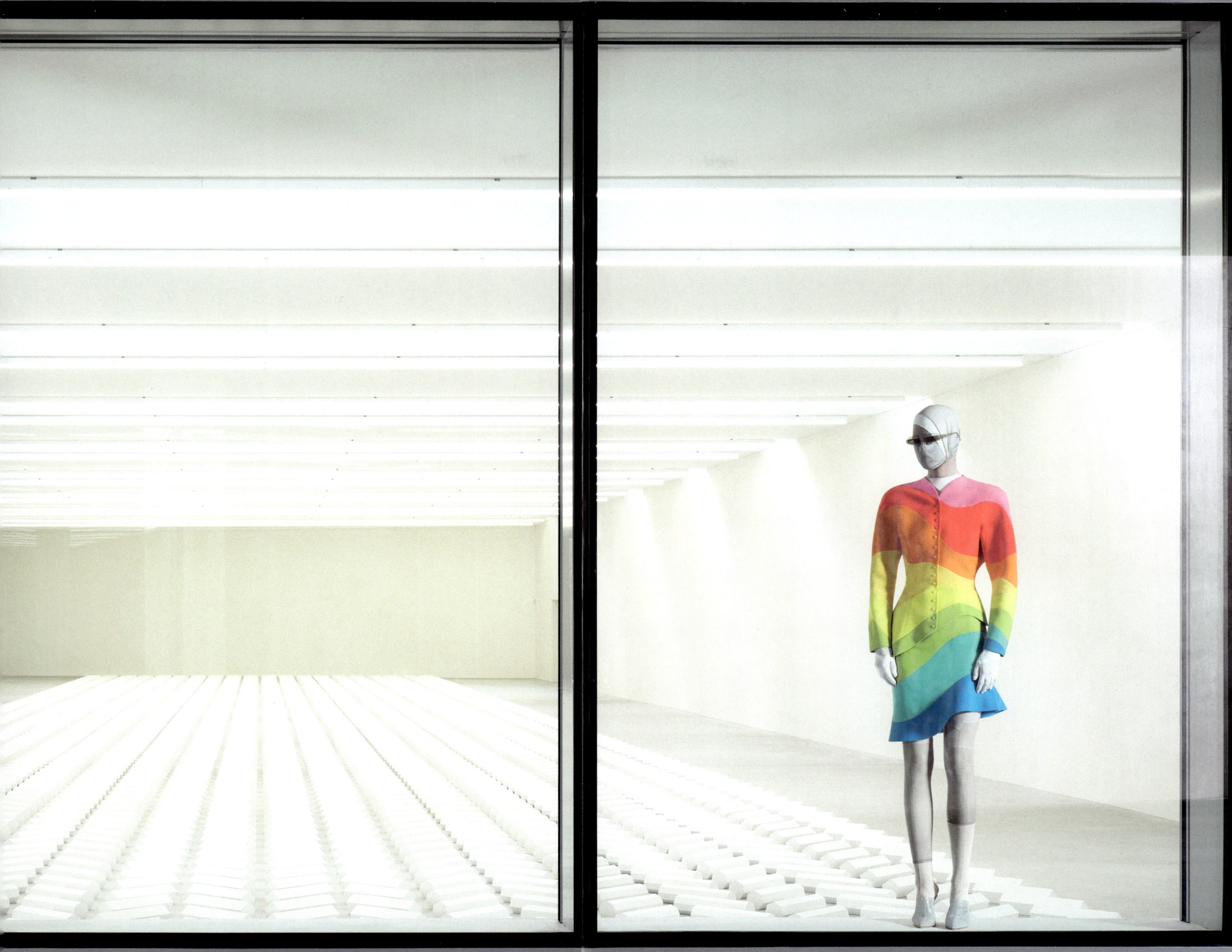

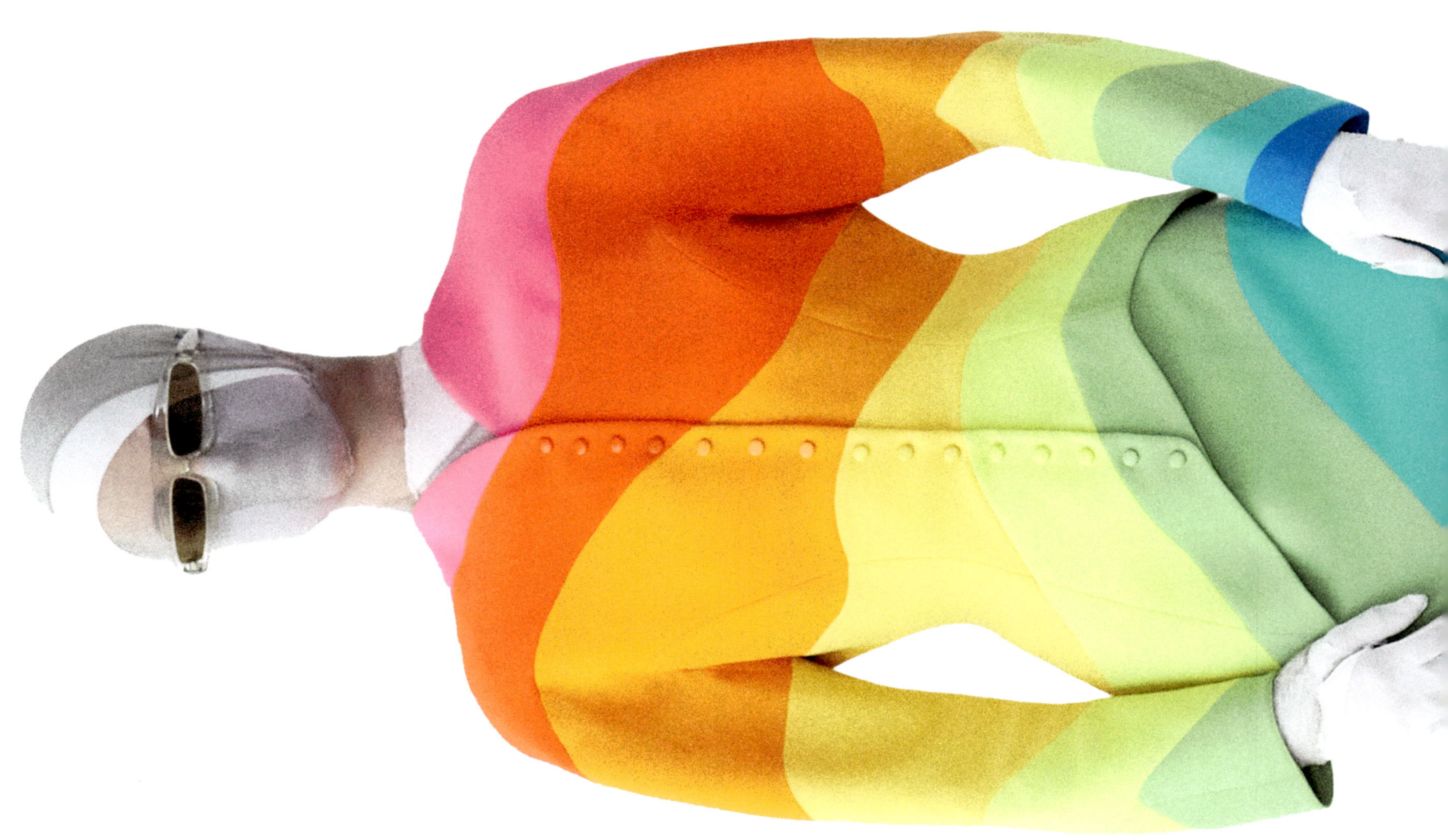

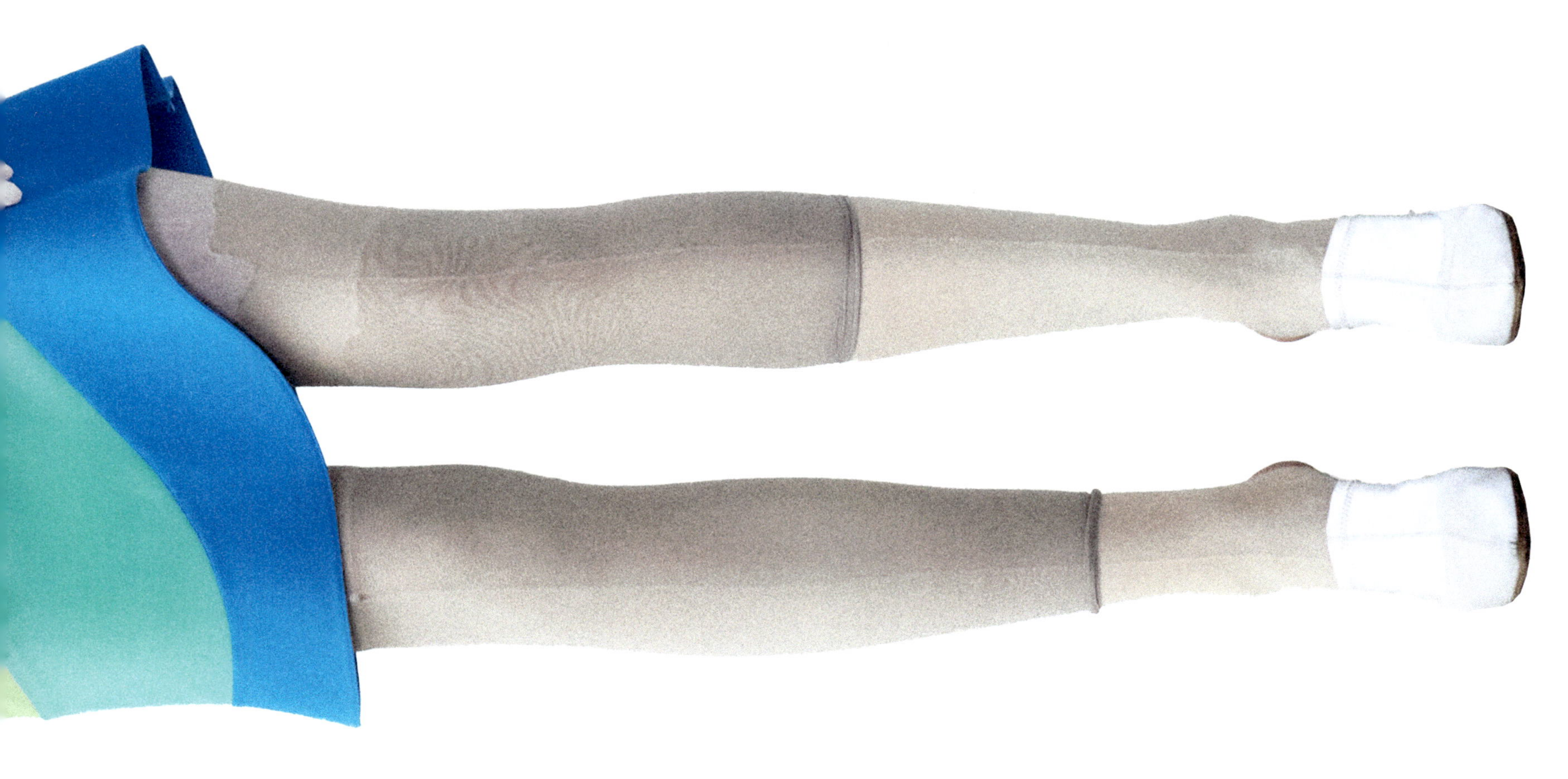

When computer graphics launched their campaign for mass adoption: the 3Dification of the screen, a nascent Virtual Reality. But strangely anachronistic for fashion; a crude 1990s technology rendering the smooth, malleable body as prismatic, rigid, stubborn. The impossible fit of computer-generated imagery (CGI) clothing: the peplum of this white Mugler jacket appears as polyhedron. An analogy to be made here with mechanical standardization. To ascend the porous, leaky body through angular flat planes. We wear these to avoid the body's mutability, its "death drive." ML

Thierry Mugler

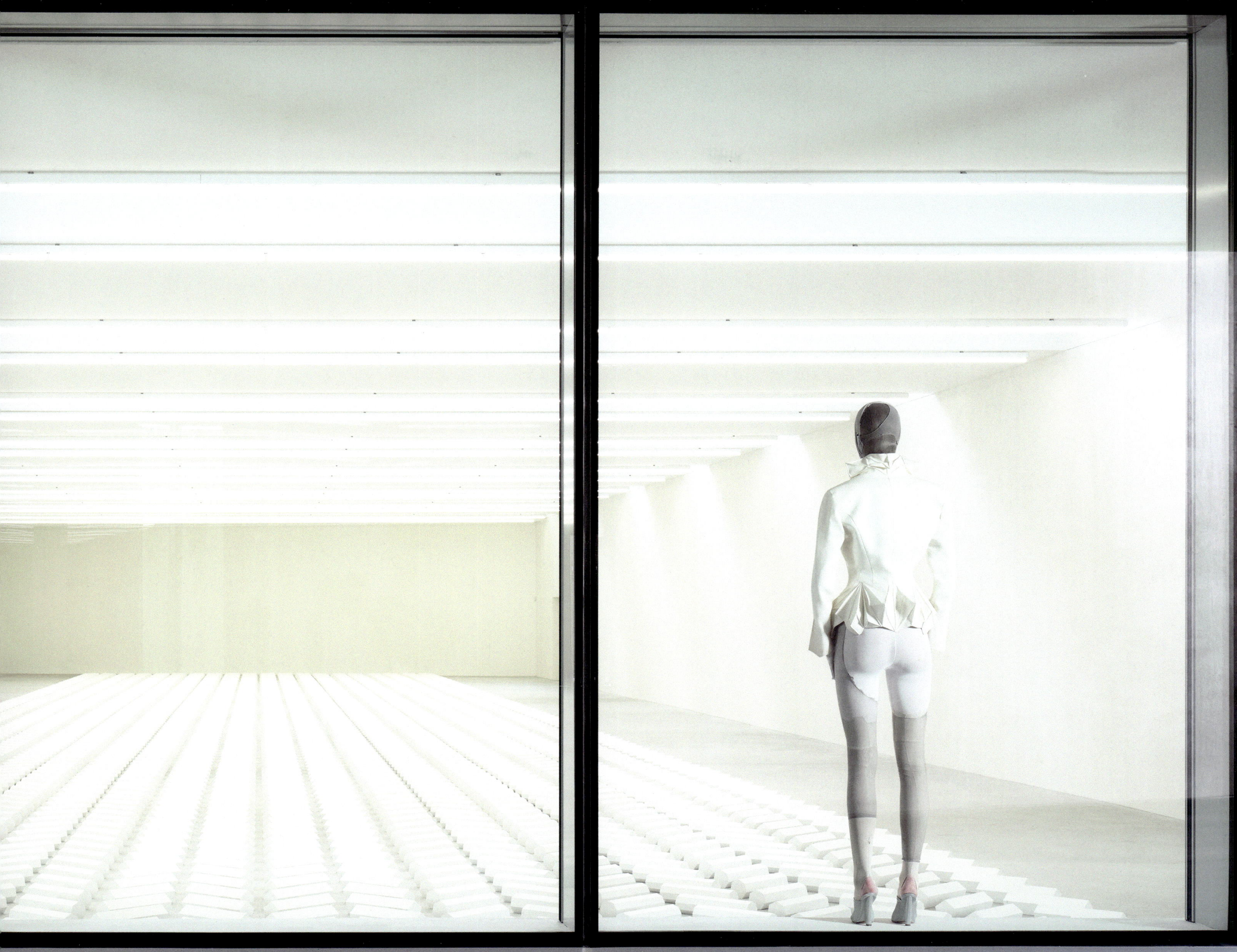

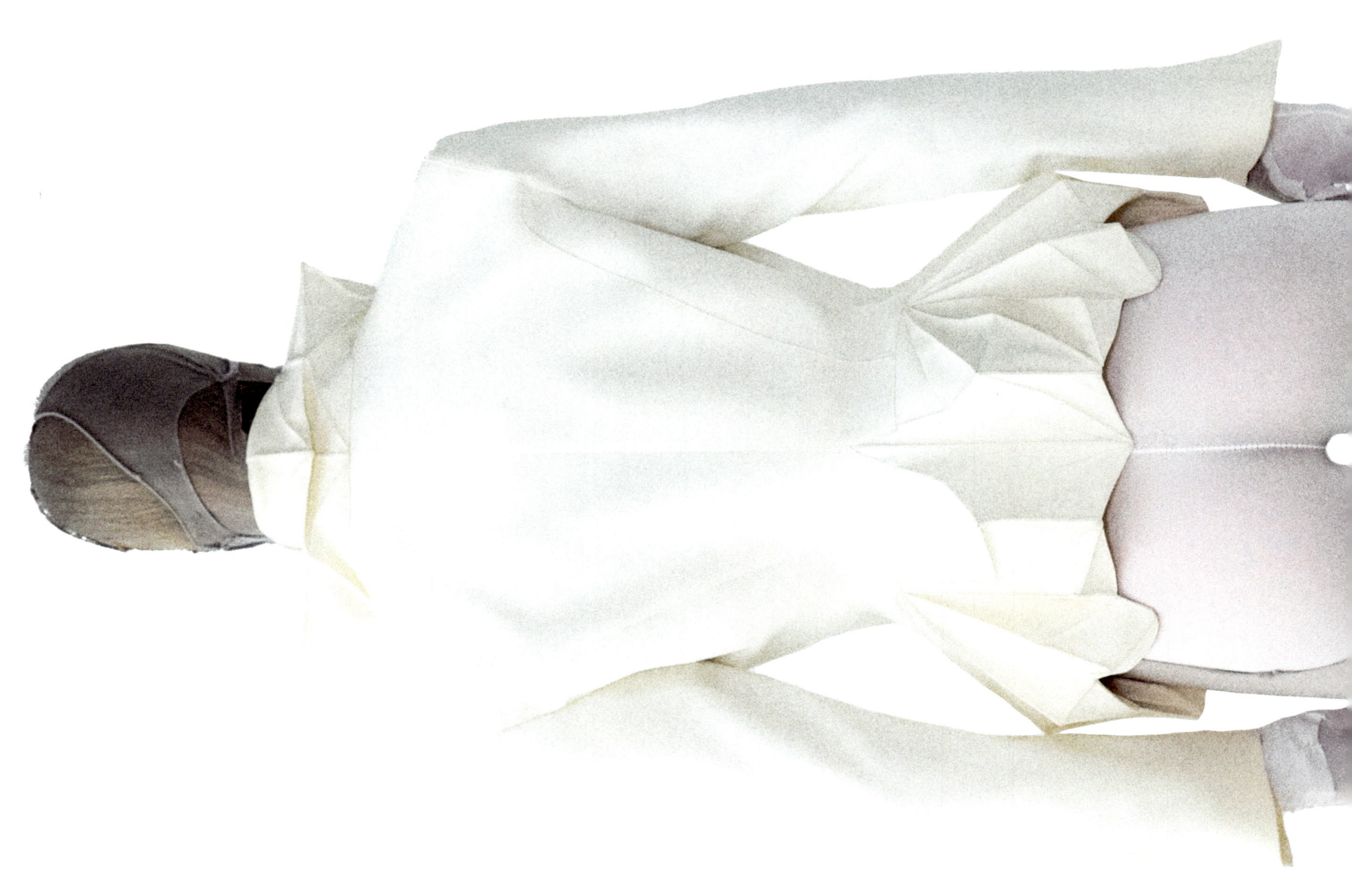

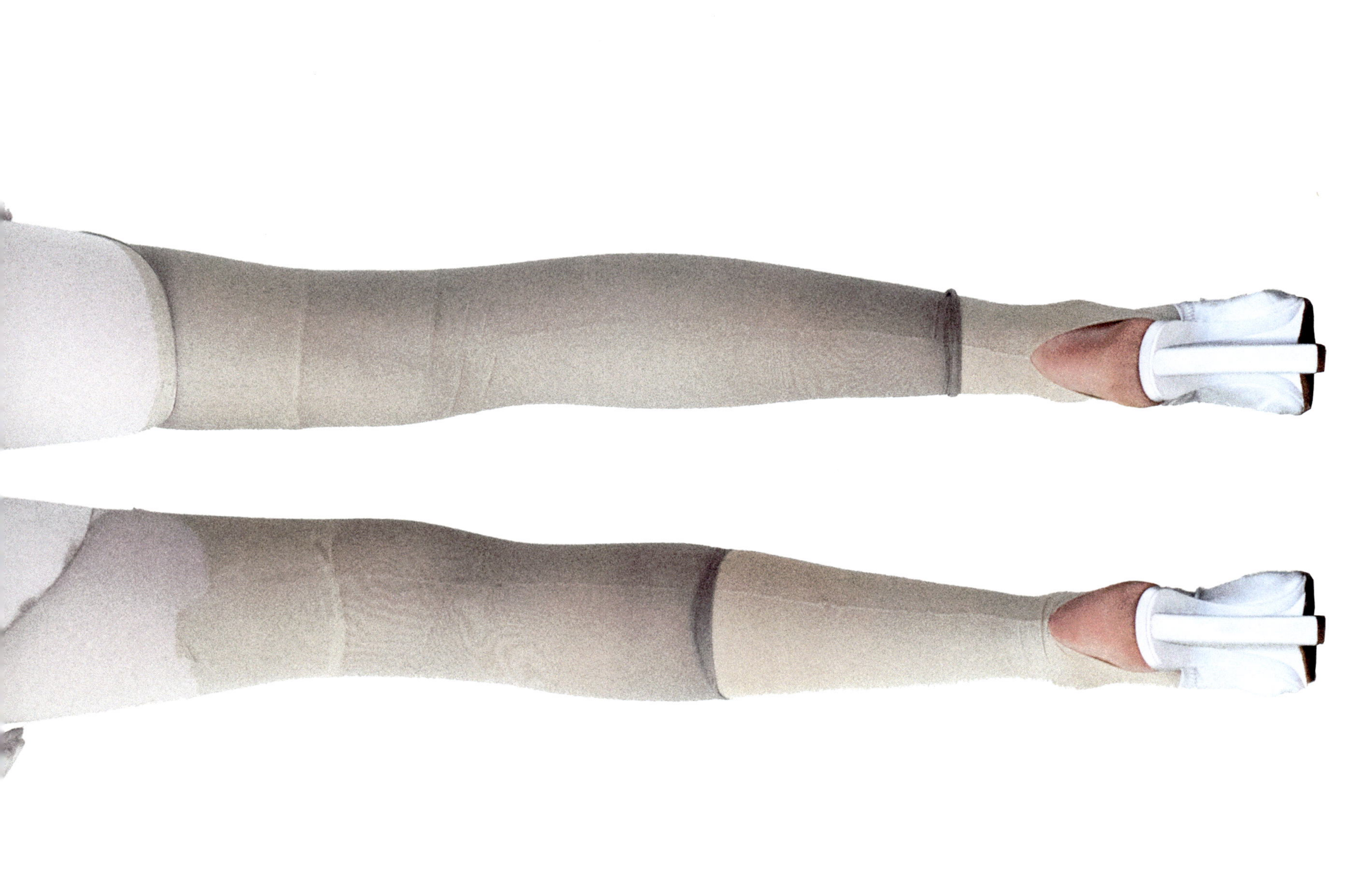

Thierry Mugler jacket, Spring/Summer 1990. Thick black jersey is applied with strips of black vinyl curved to accentuate the waist. The edge-stitched vinyl is spiked at either end forming a neck ruff and feathered hem. The appeal of a biotech petroleum congealing android and animal. Such dark metamorphosis a leitmotif for fashion's turn of the decade: from the halcyon 1980s lucre of deregulated finance, Versace gold, and Sex & Suits into the 1990s poète maudit, heroin overdose, and grunge androgyny. ML

Thierry Mugler
Spring/Summer 1990

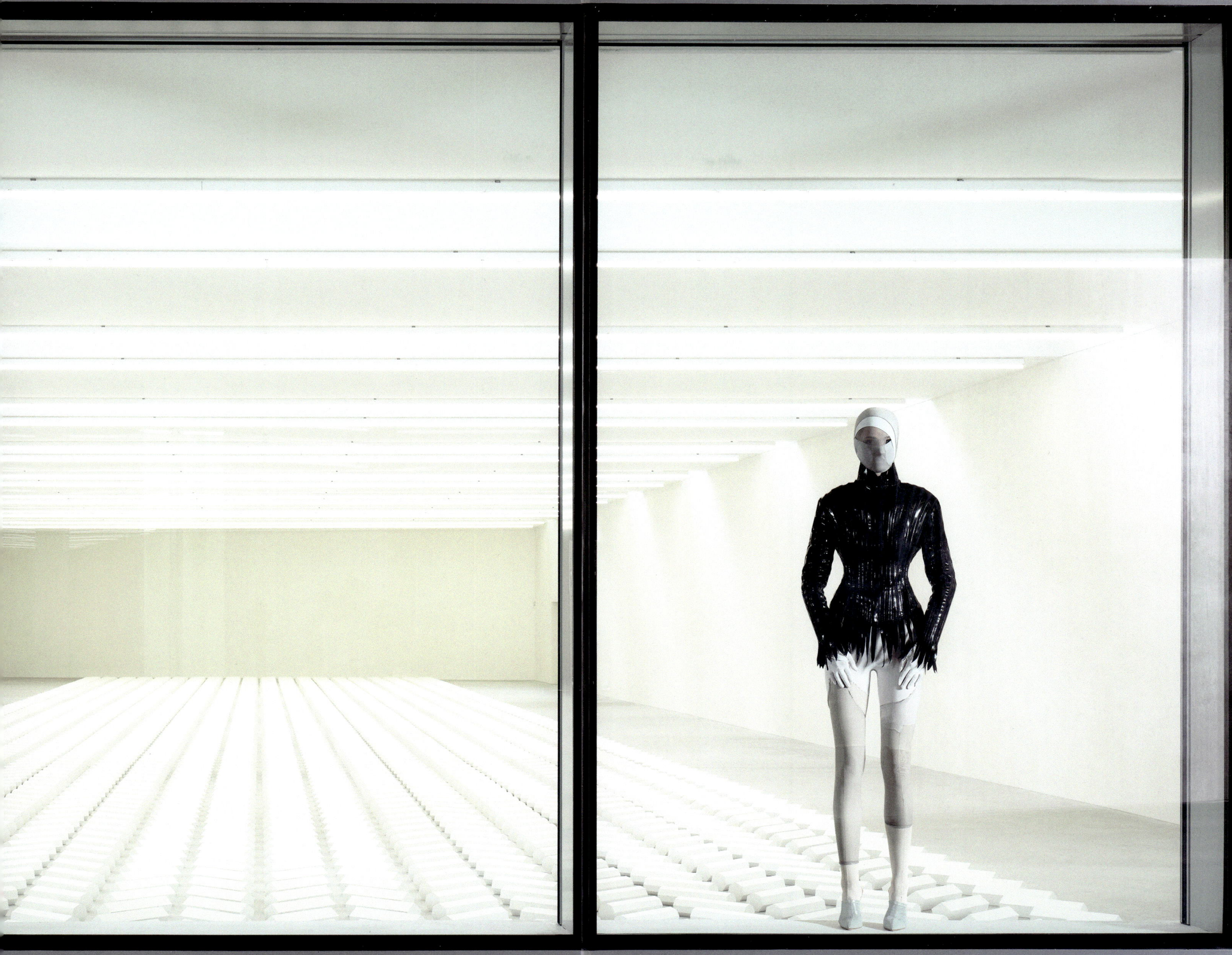

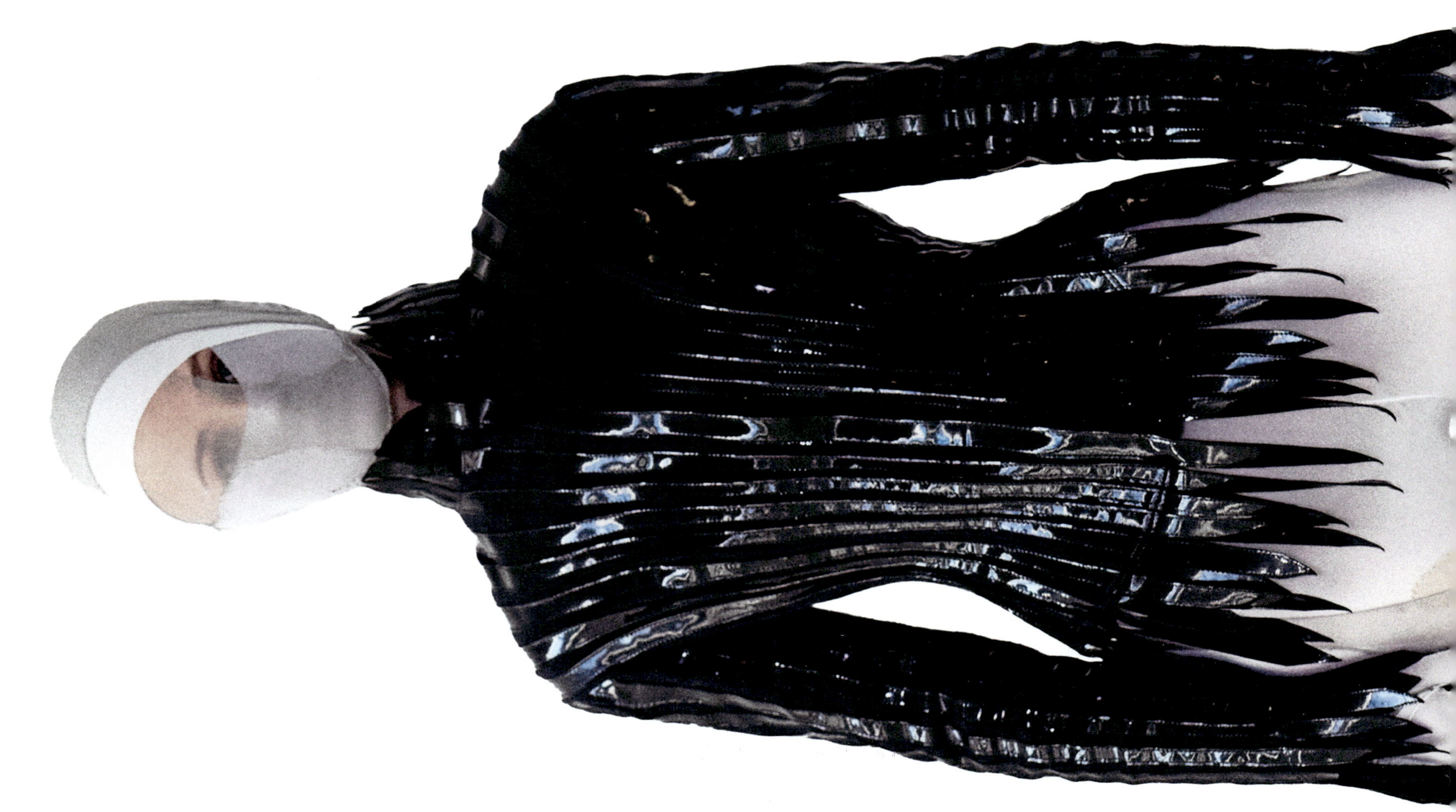

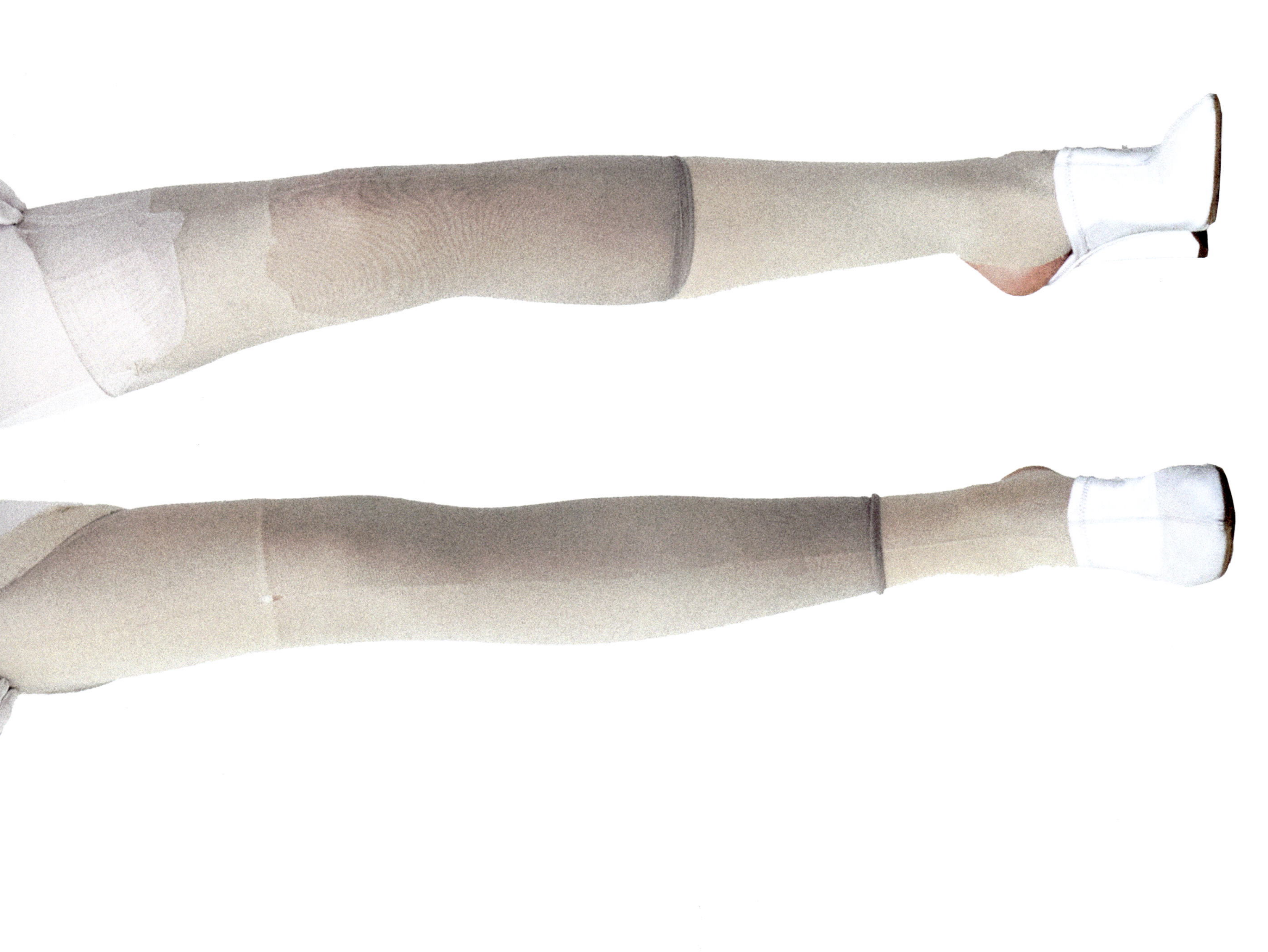

Theatricality was never lost on French fashion designer Thierry Mugler. The Spring/Summer 1992 collection, titled *Les Cowboys*, paraded a camp pastiche of cowpoke chaps, Vegas showgirls, Mae West look-alikes, and his canonical Harley Davidson bustier: a sculptural showpiece almost preordained for museum display. Also featured in the collection is a version of this golden sequin tuxedo with shawl lapel, cropped to suggest a tailcoat. ML

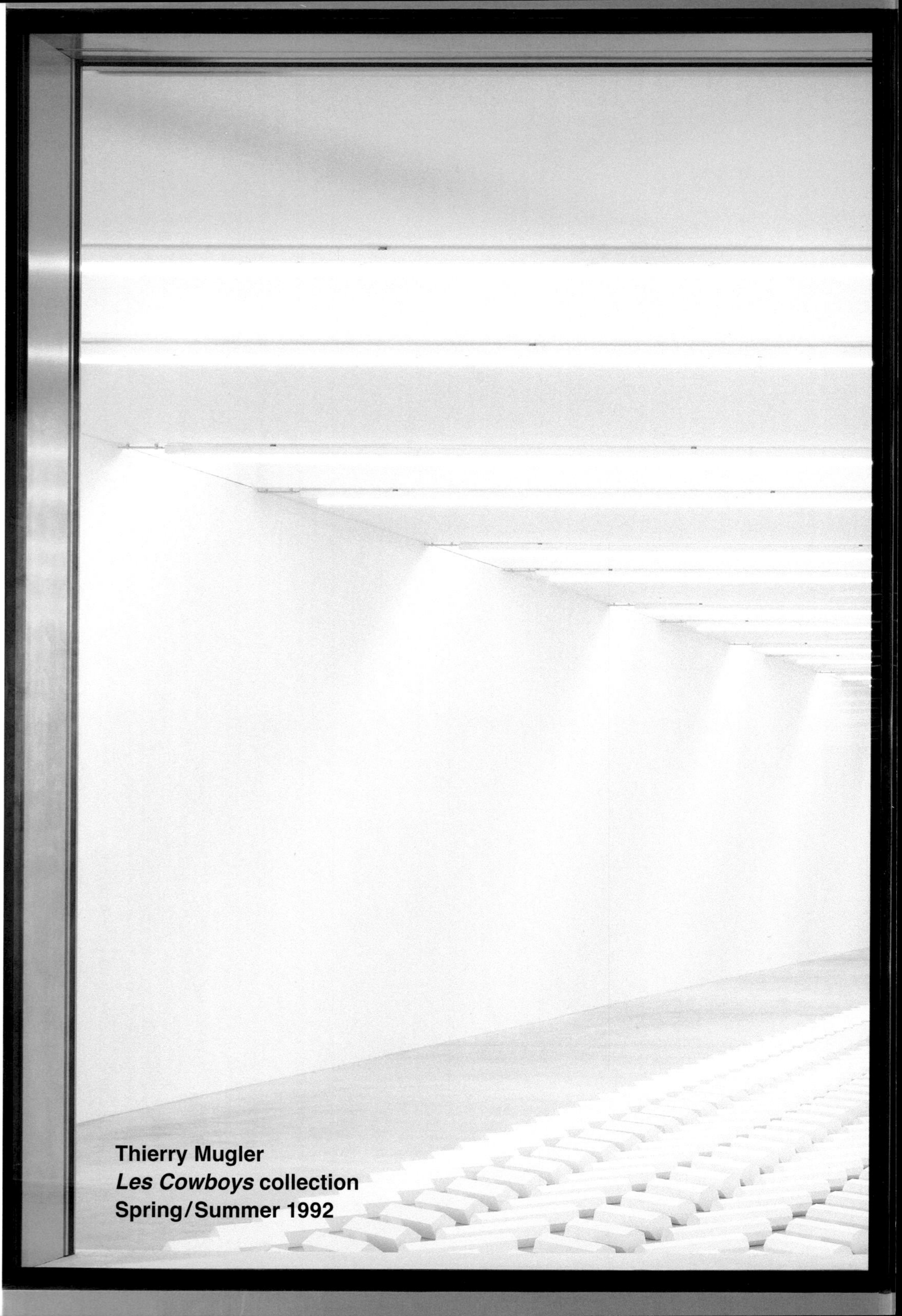

Thierry Mugler
Les Cowboys collection
Spring/Summer 1992

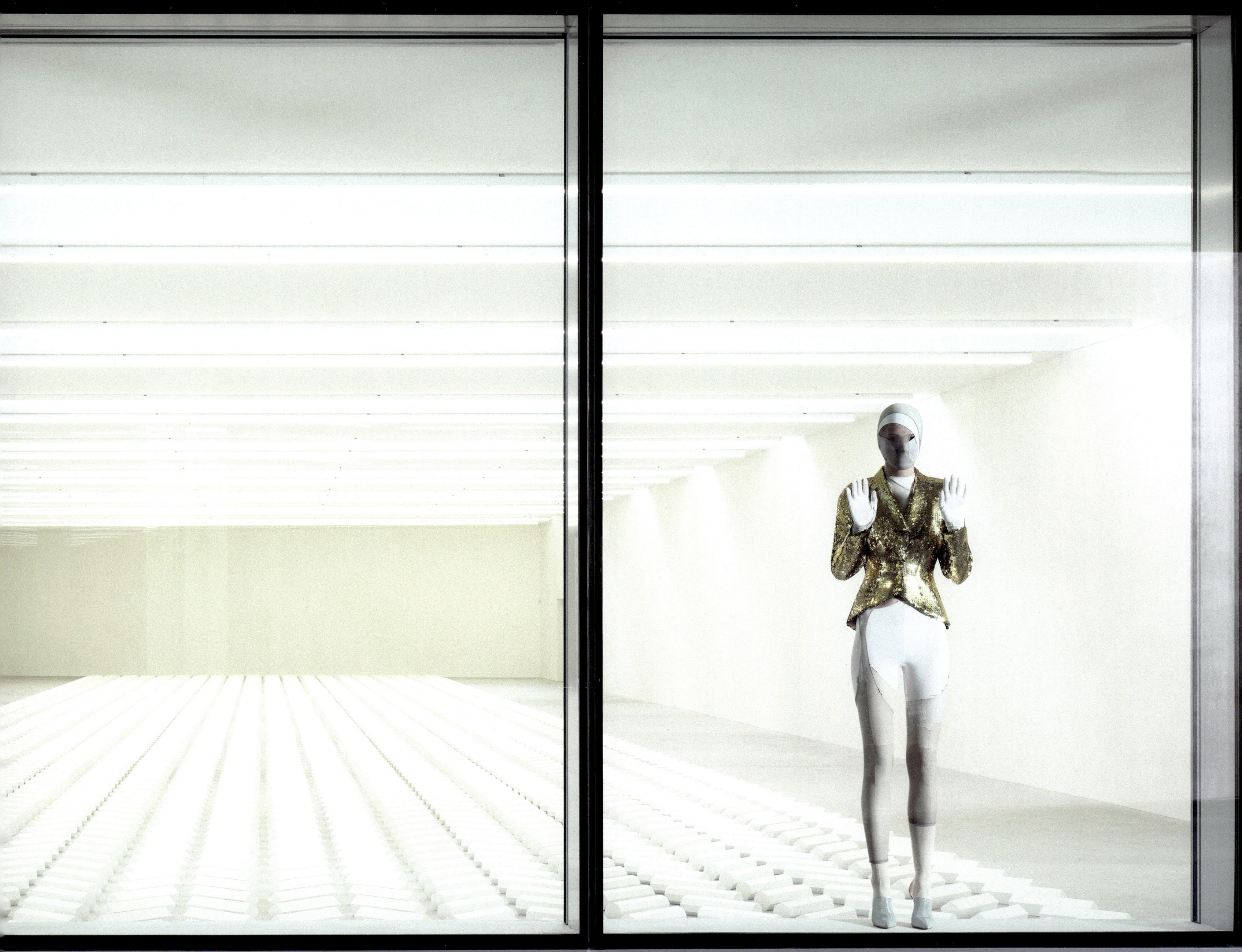

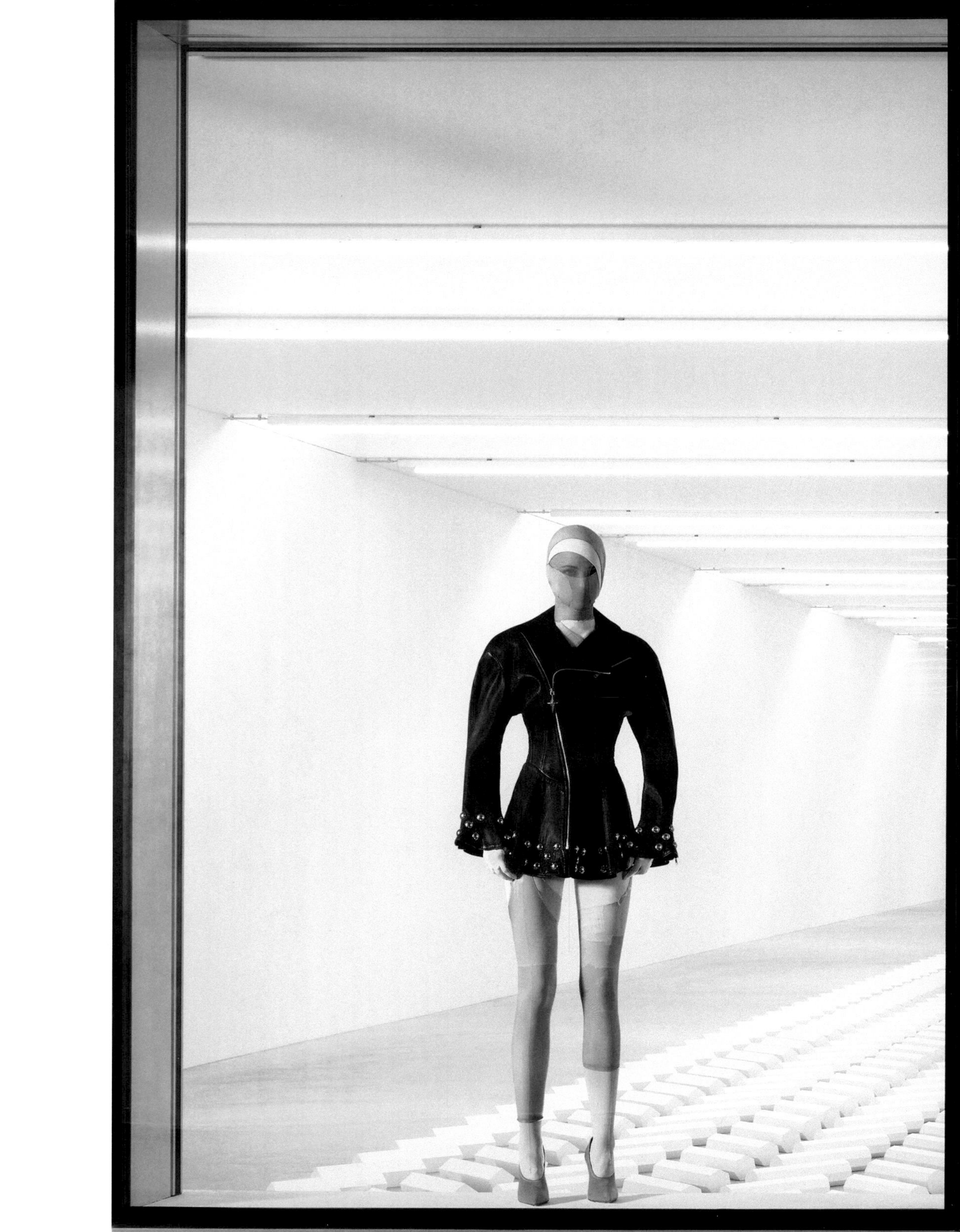

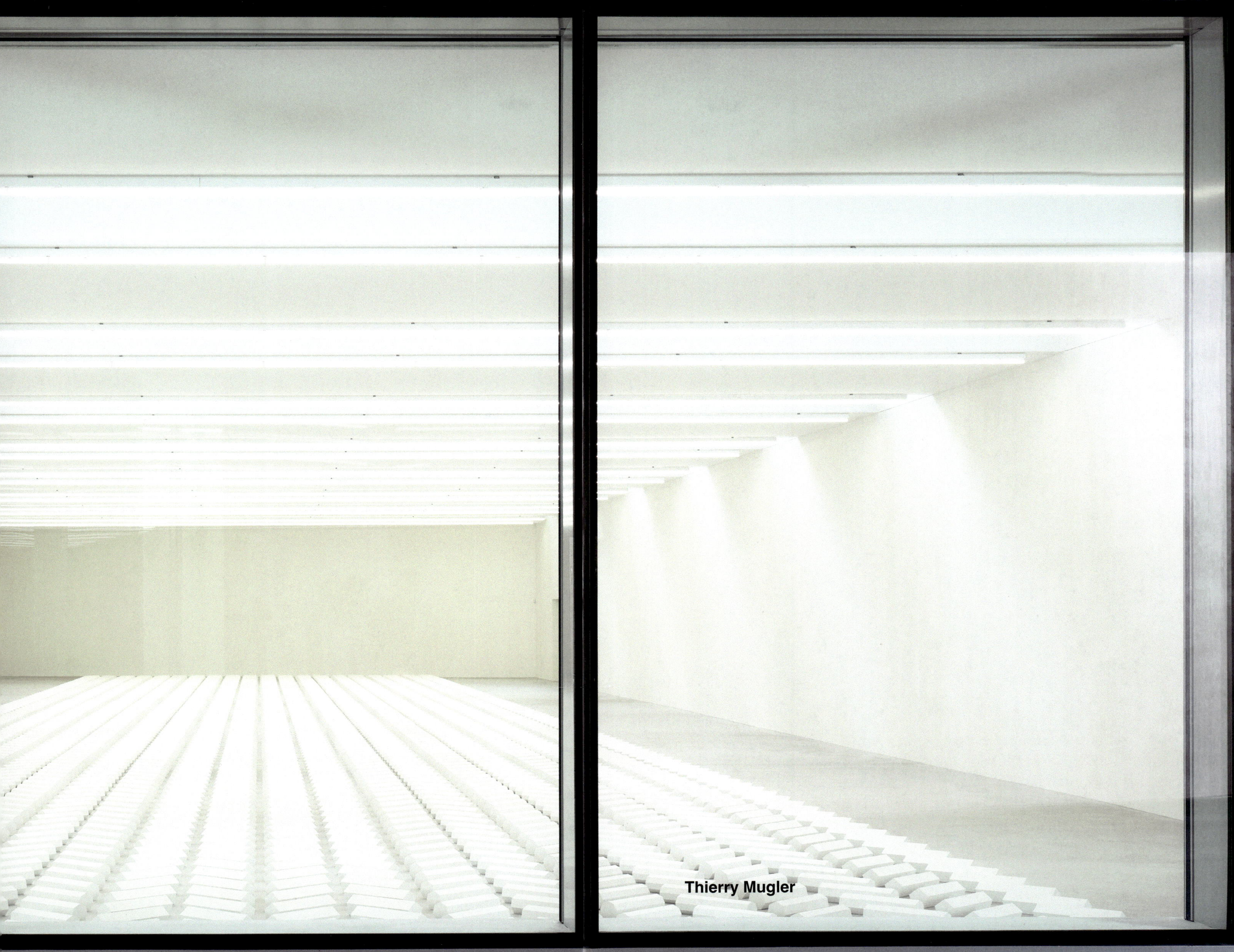
Thierry Mugler

This double-breasted jet-black jacket from Mugler's Fall/ Winter 1989/90 *Hiver Buick* collection features a flared peplum with such severe interfacing it appears as plastic mold. The piece displays an ostentatious lapidary of gemstones in vivid artificial coloring cascading the shoulder and chest. Models Willi Ninja, Iman, and Adrian Alicea are seen voguing these on the runway. A camp, amphetamine-fueled fête galante. ML

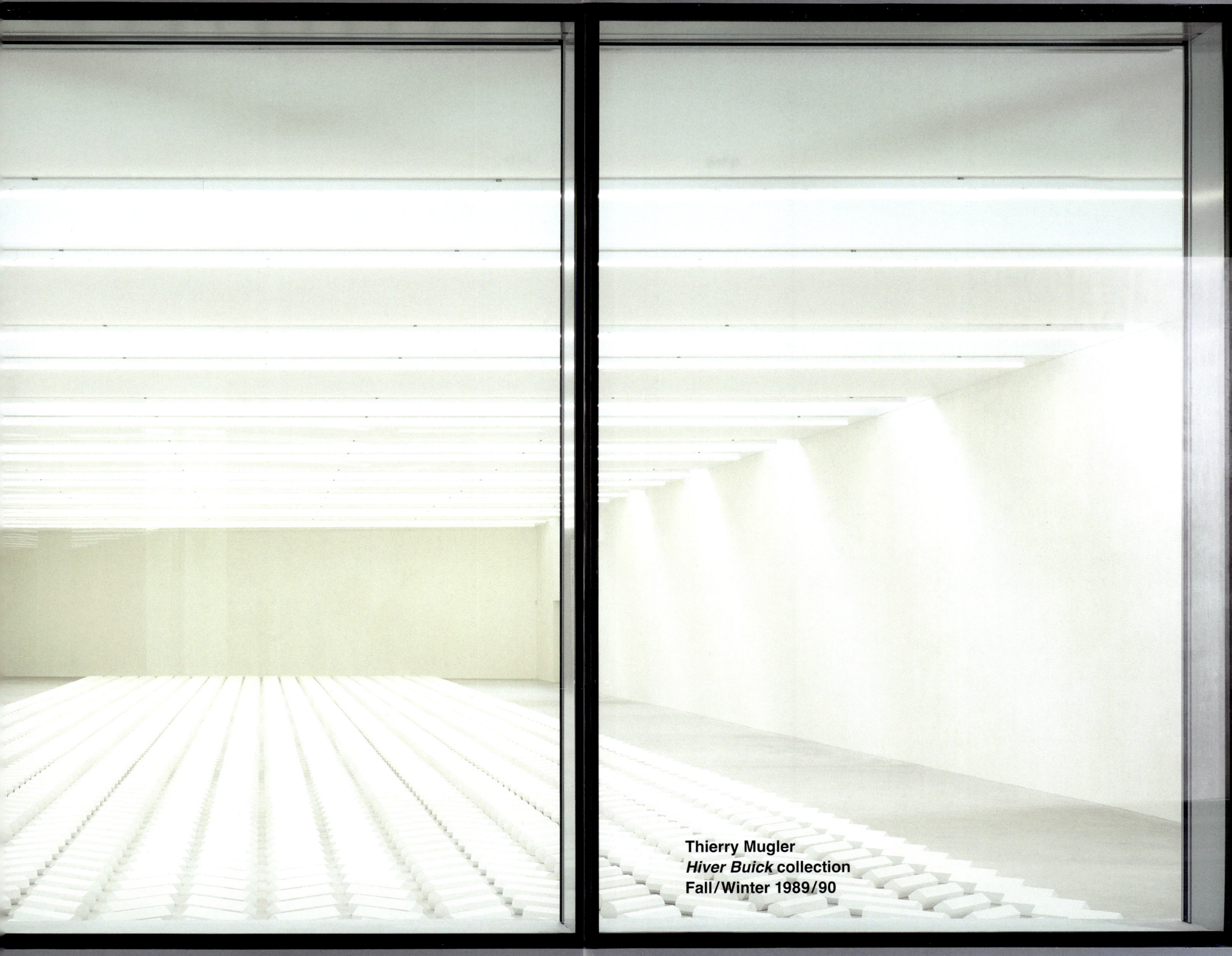

Thierry Mugler
Hiver Buick collection
Fall/Winter 1989/90

The soft goth succubus, private equity investor. This Thierry Mugler purple suit jacket features a scalloped hem, cuffs, and peaked lapel with raised collar. ML

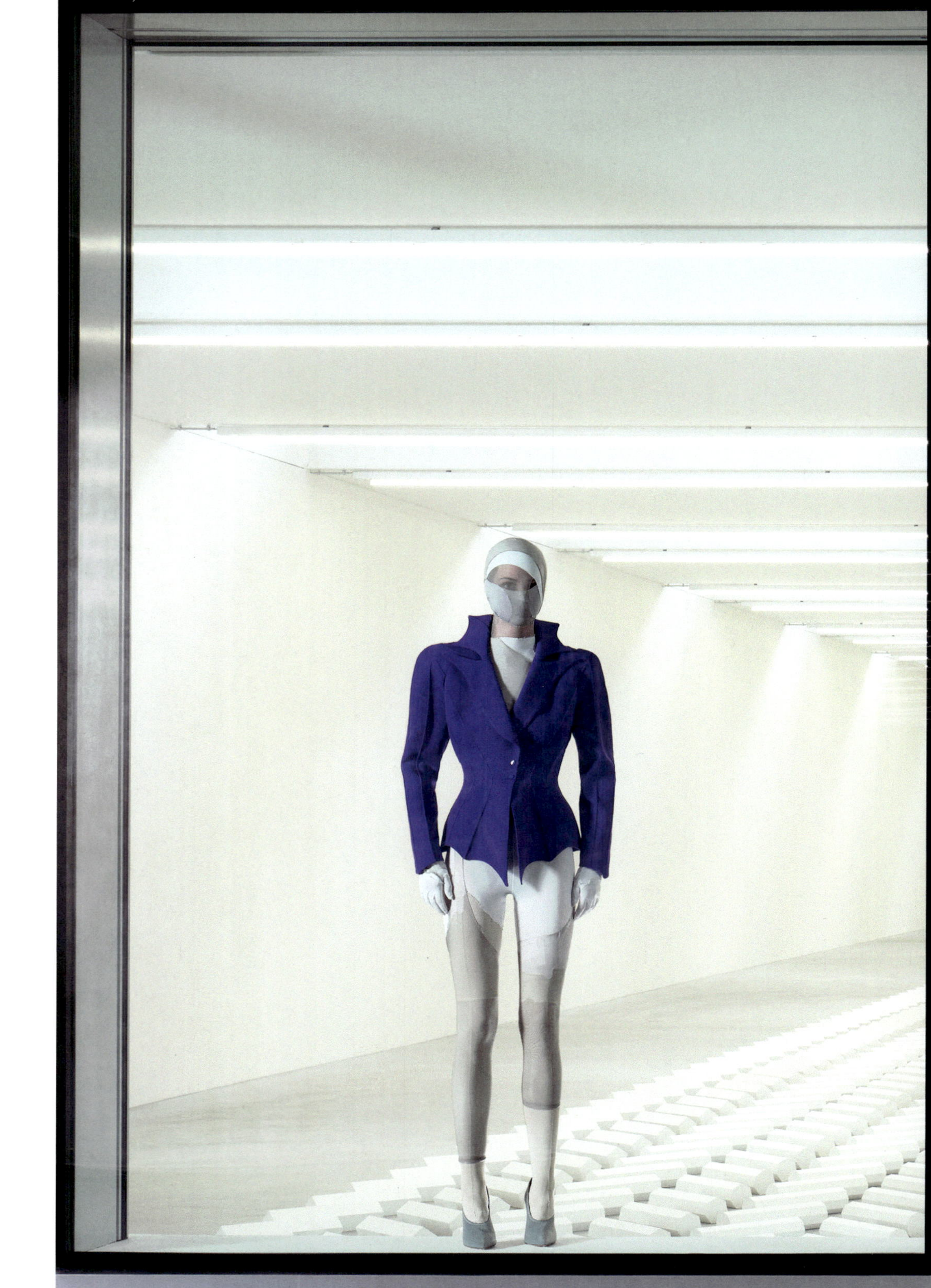

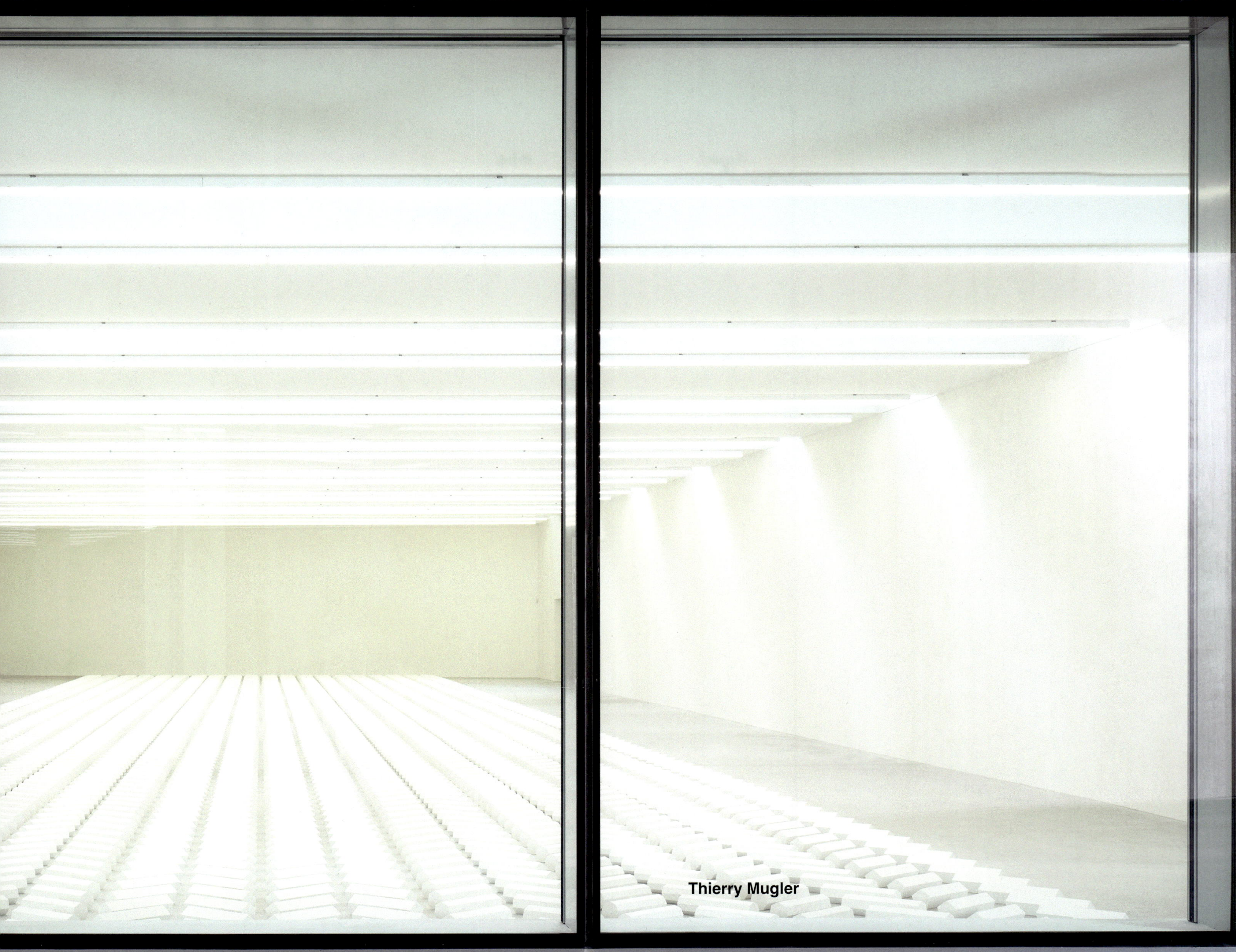
Thierry Mugler

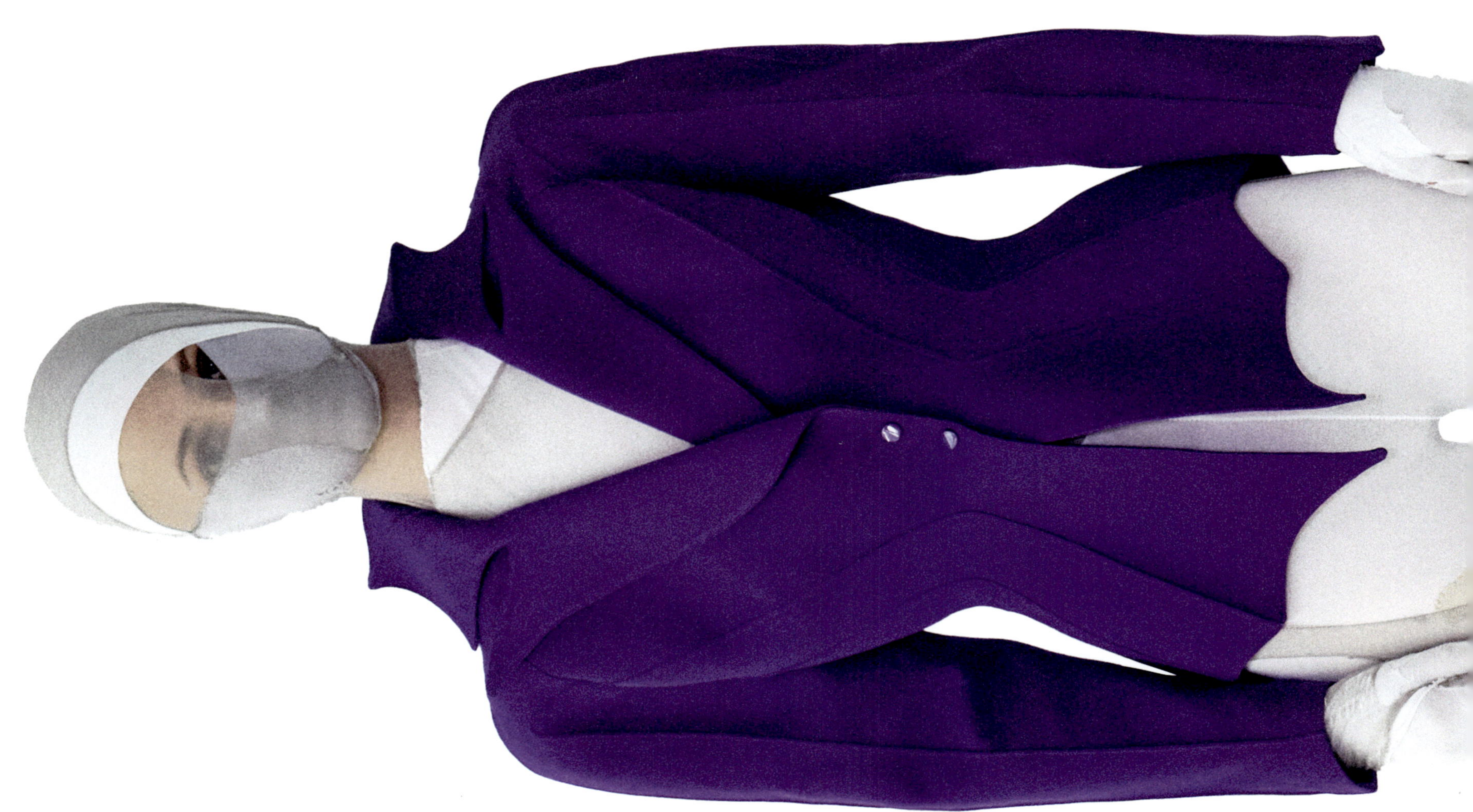

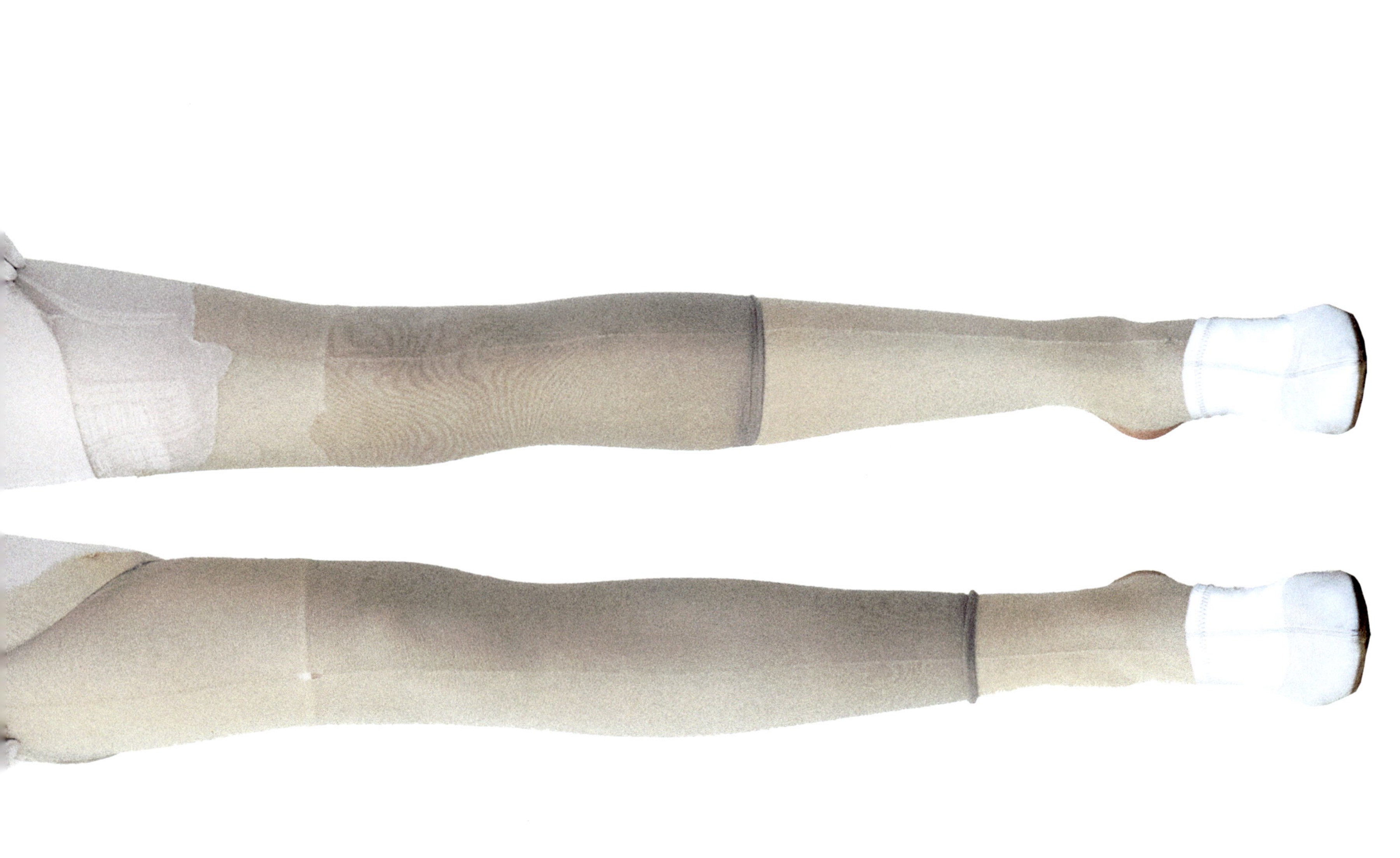

Leather as our supreme fetish. The sexual kink of applying smooth, durable deceased animal skin on our own. Motorcycles, Tom of Finland, BDSM. Thierry Mugler's motorcycle jacket from Fall/Winter 1989/90 *Hiver Buick* collection features a Cadillac grill accent, motorcycle seat detailing, and upholstered padding. ML

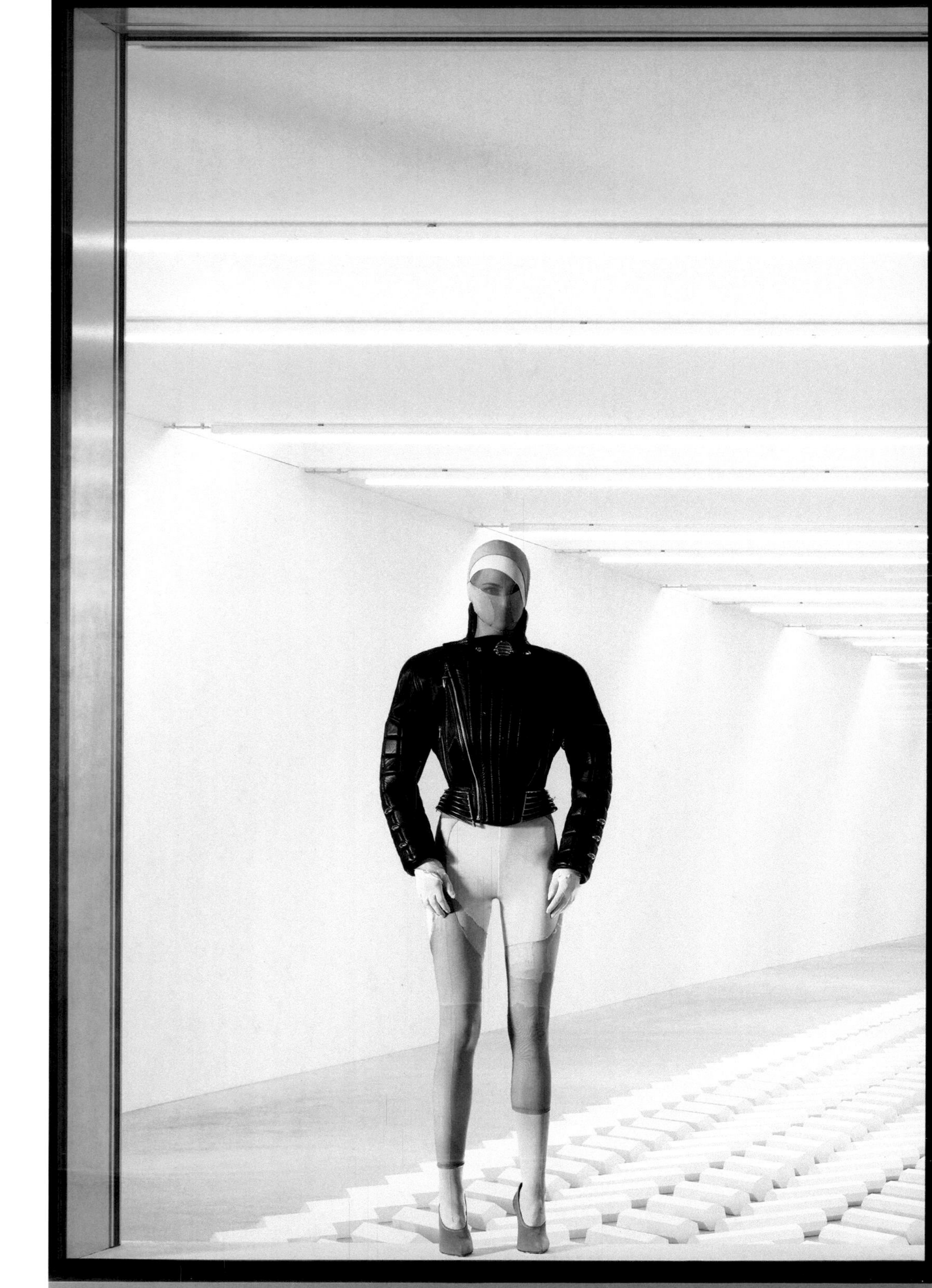

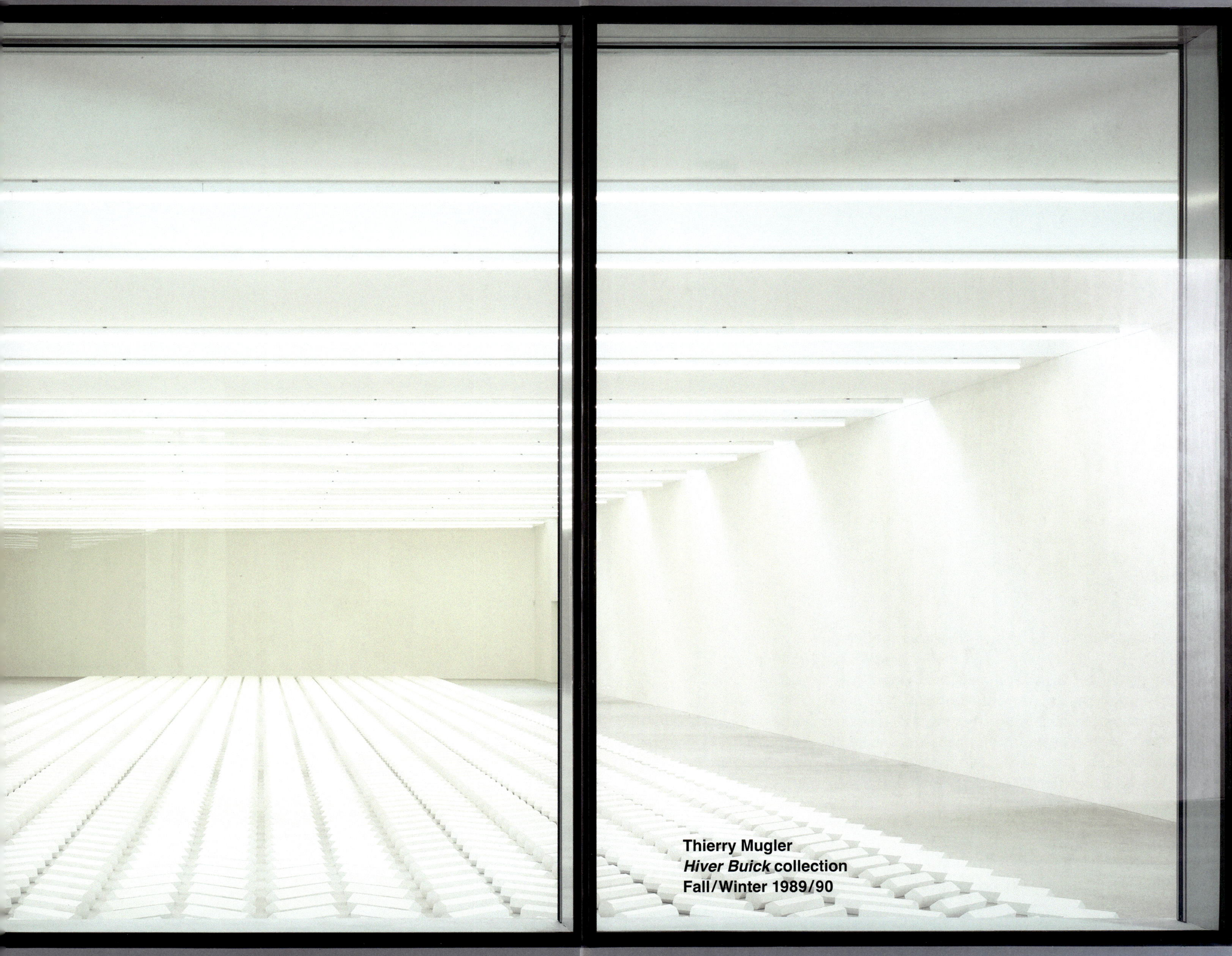

Thierry Mugler
Hiver Buick collection
Fall/Winter 1989/90

Thierry Mugler was known for hyperbolic femininity, an eroticized superwoman expressing a perfected and invincible plastic form. Mugler's woman is manifestly futuristic: technological and powerfully phallic. A future also obsessed with a certain zoophilia: erotizing non-human animals, like insects and reptiles, as anthropomorphized suits, dresses, and eyewear (most notably his Spring/Summer 1997 *Les Insectes* collection). This Spring/Summer 1991 PVC jacket prods our animalistic fetish. By scoring double layered PVC in a diamond pattern, a snakeskin scale effect is produced. The 3D modified fabric is fitted tight to body. The side seams are laced, binding the figure to the fashion historical feminine iconography of corsetry. ML

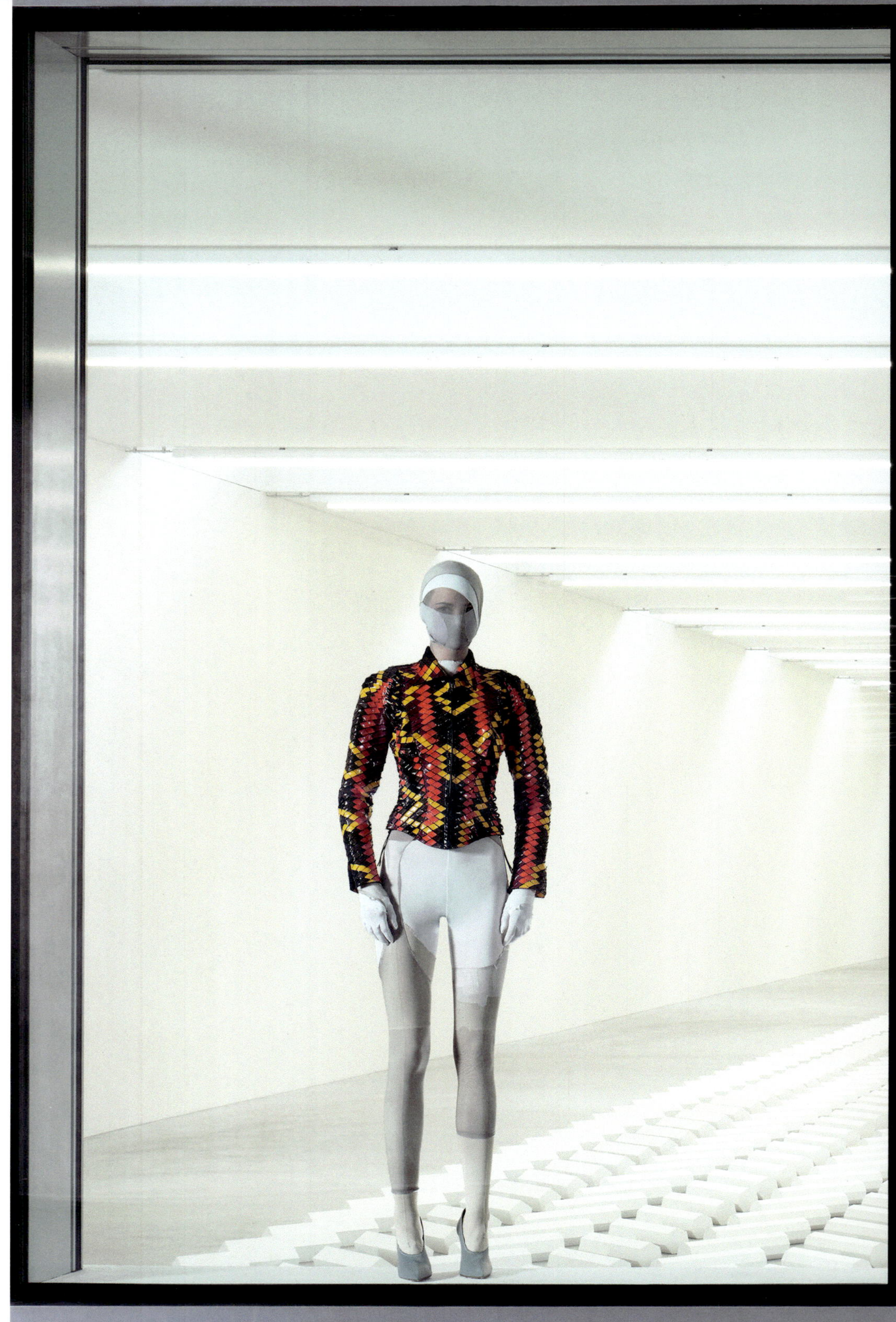

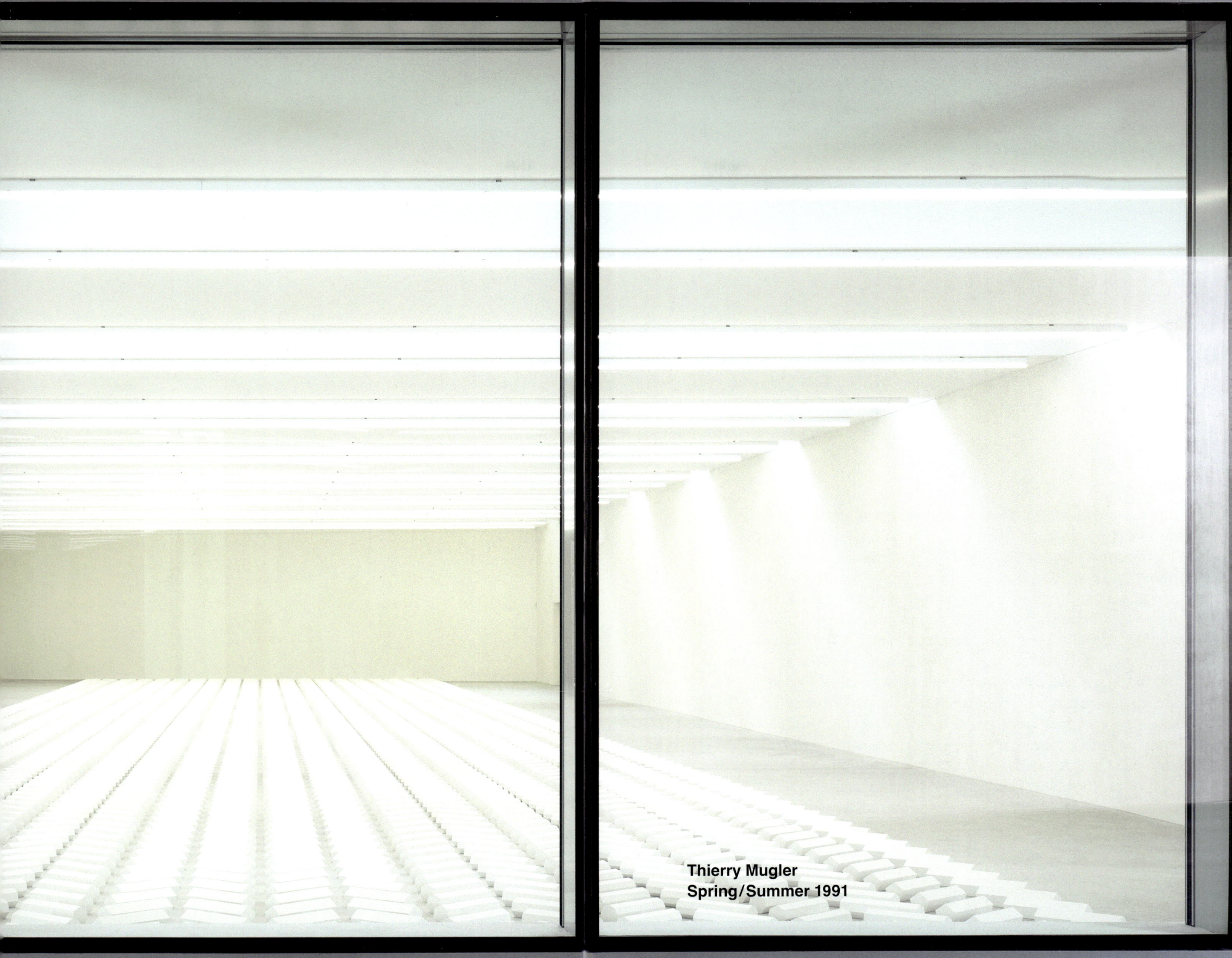

Thierry Mugler
Spring/Summer 1991

This canonical waisted jacket with zipper closure and mandarin collar from Thierry Mugler's Fall/Winter 1990/91 *Anatomique Computer* collection resembles the early innovations of computer-generated imagery (CGI): a Cartesian plane of 2D rasterized neon lines simulating the direction of space. Comprised of a black rayon cotton blend velveteen with plastic cord trim, the piece maps, à la Tron, the algorithmic curvatures of an idealized woman's figure: busty and taut. Debuted upon the dawn of the century's finale decade, appearing as harbinger (or omen) of various nascent technosocial upheavals: the digitized proliferation of financialization; of cyberfeminism, CCRU, VR; and stimming, synthetics, and body-modding. Conflating as Mugler's ideal of an "unnatural body," as he once put it. The vectorization of beauty. Think of early Lara Croft, polygonal and rigid, whose evolution eventuates into the smooth curvature of contemporary CGI. This is our cargo cult, one impossible to separate from a primitive, libidinal drive. Our first cyborgs won't be battle droids but sex dolls. ML

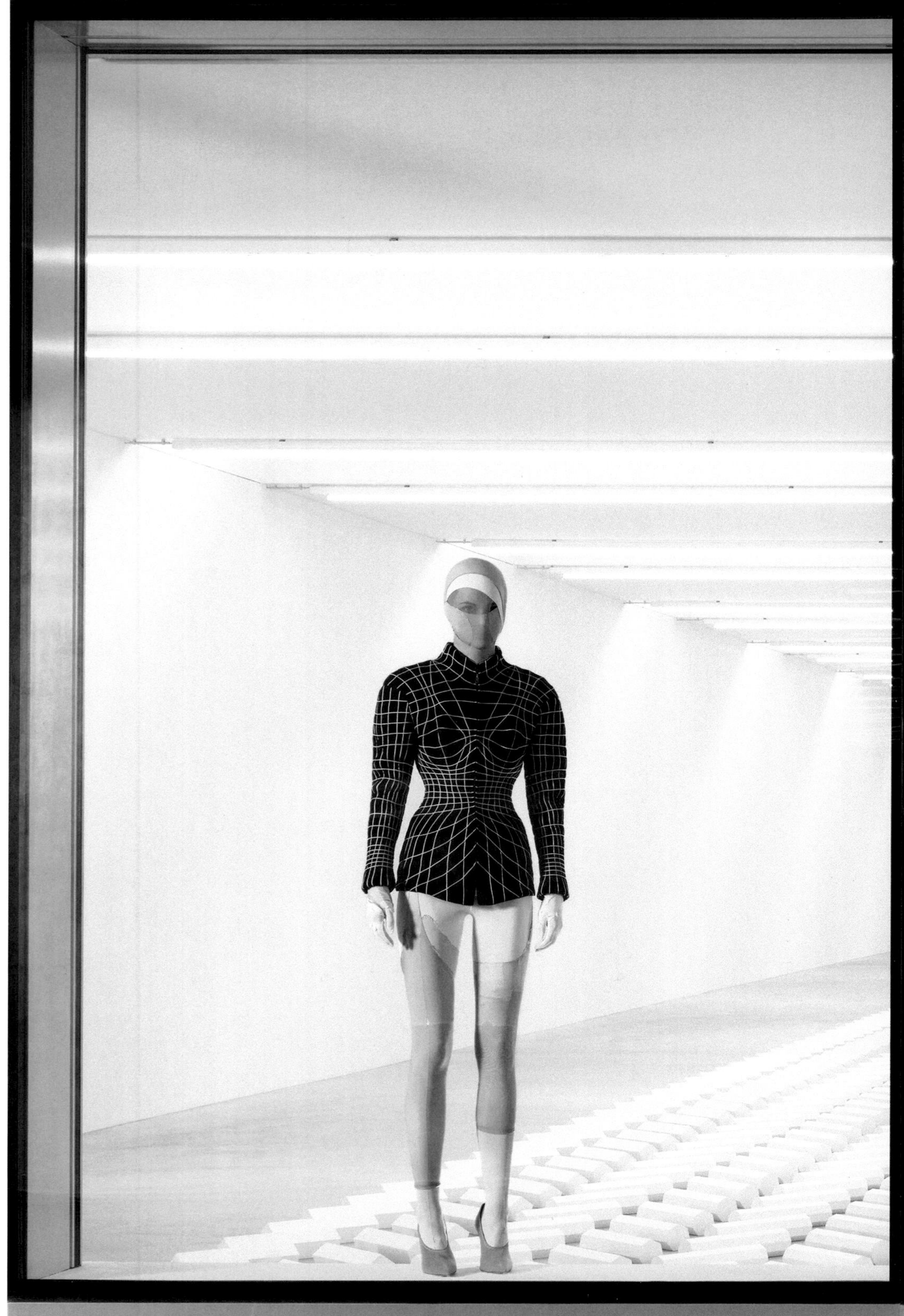

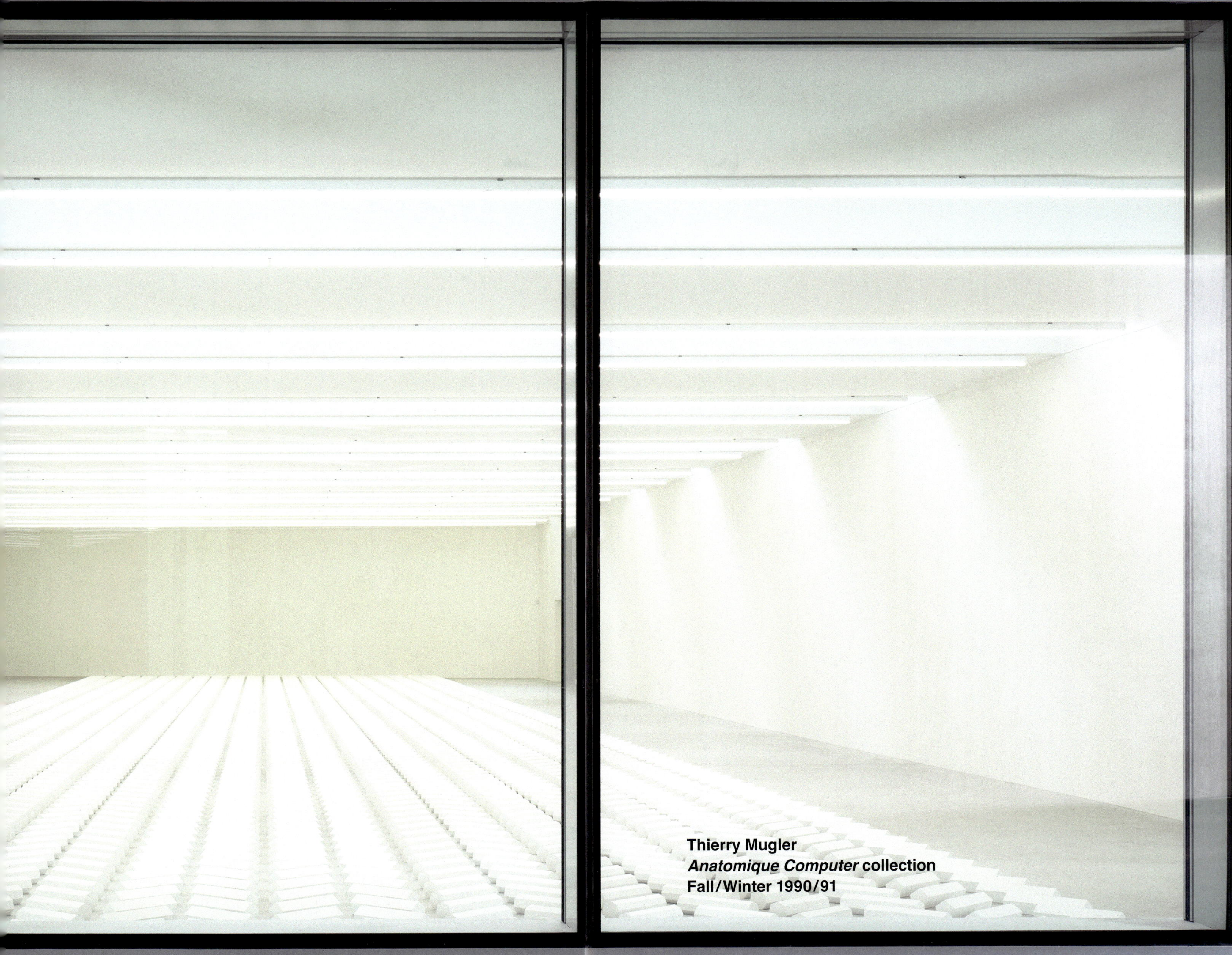

Thierry Mugler
Anatomique Computer collection
Fall/Winter 1990/91

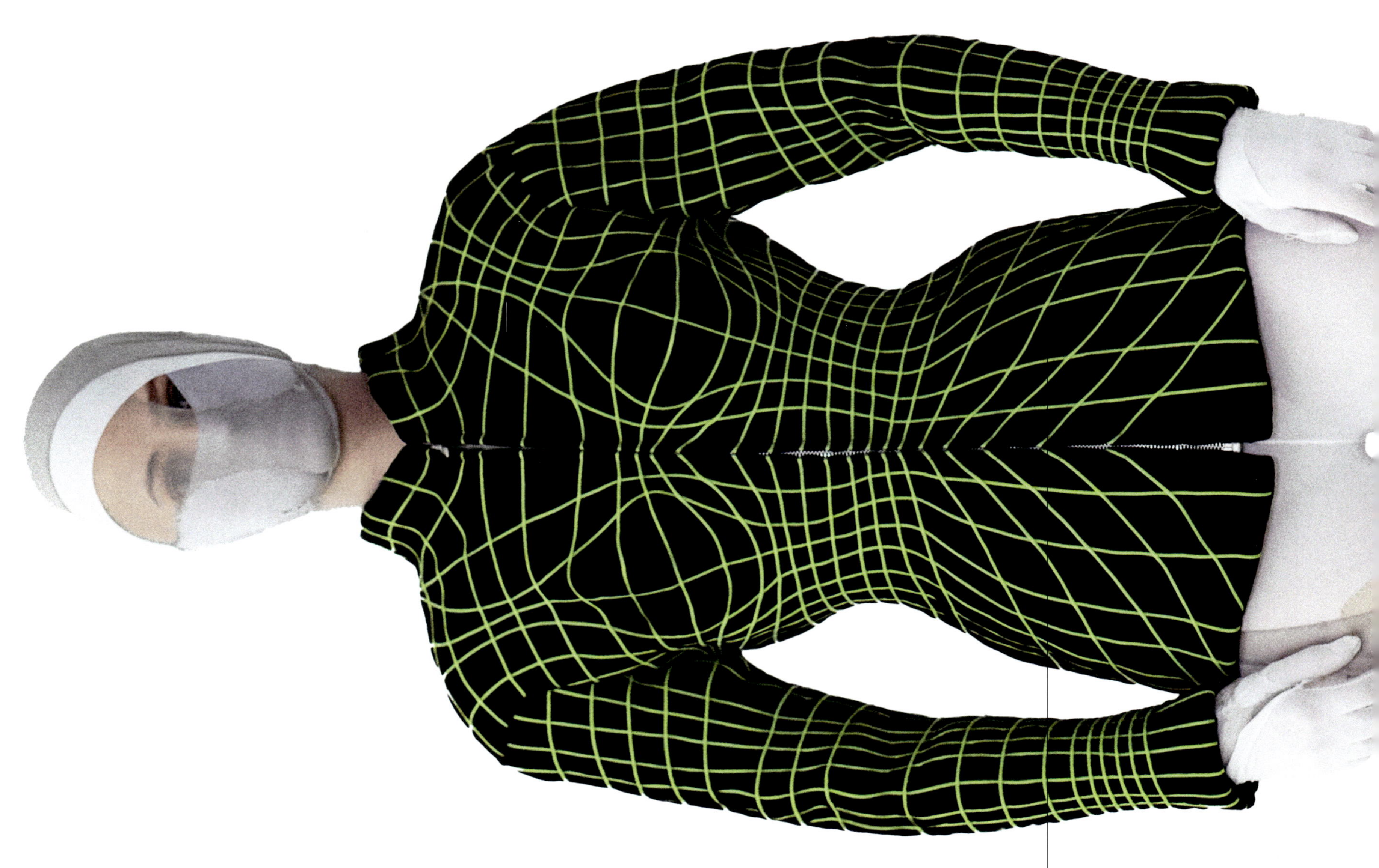

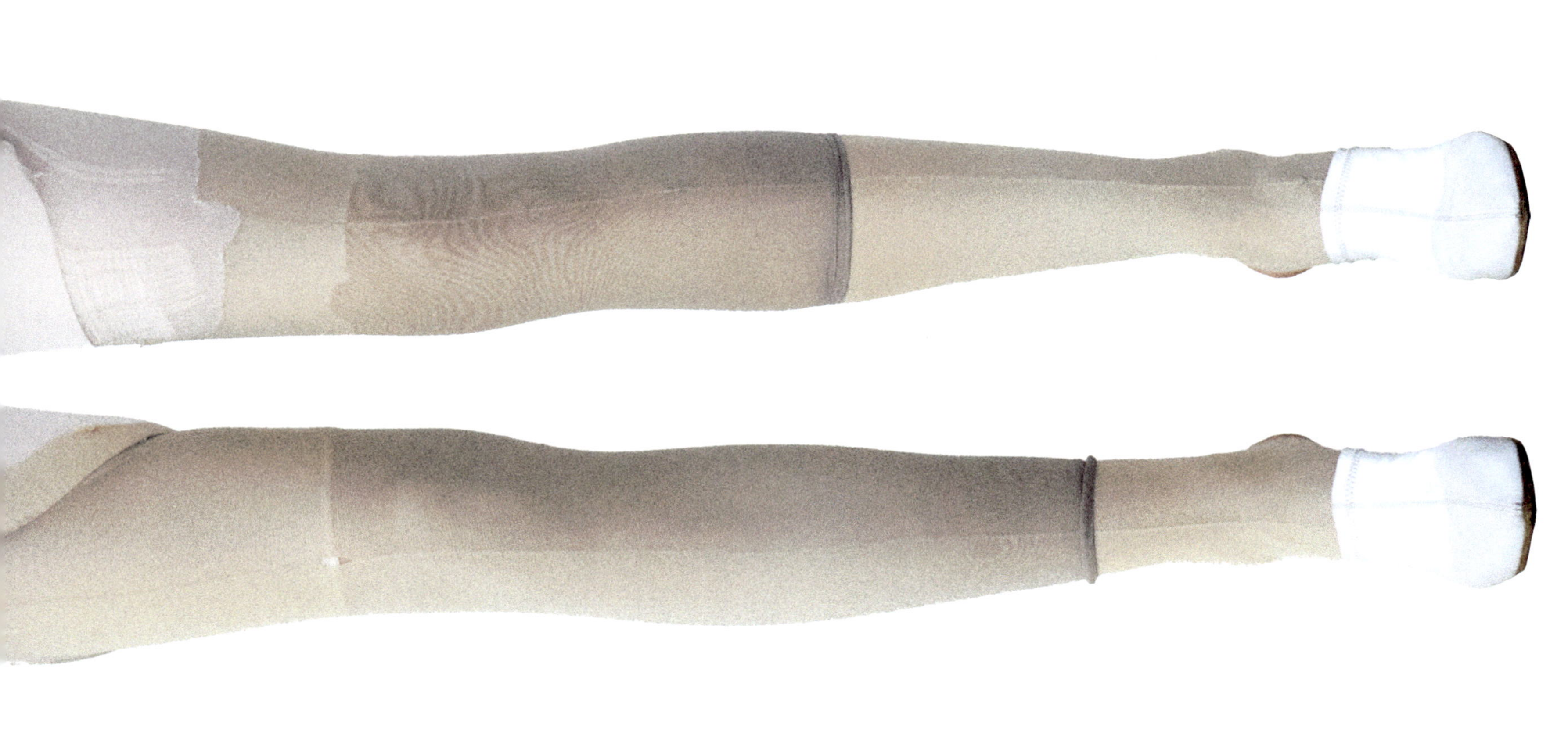

A Thierry Mugler red satin evening gown with asymmetric neckline, twisted bodice, and single padded, oversized sleeve is completed by a lopsided train. His Fall/Winter 1986/87 collection *Hiver Russe*, meaning Russian Winter, much like the Yves Saint Laurent and Jean Paul Gaultier collections of the same season, sent Soviet-inspired pieces marching down their runways. While travelling the Volgograd countryside, Mugler photographed Angela Wilde posing on a 66-foot-tall crimson star. Mugler's idealized militarism captured upon the ruins of a nation state. ML

Thierry Mugler
Hiver Russe collection
Fall/Winter 1986/87

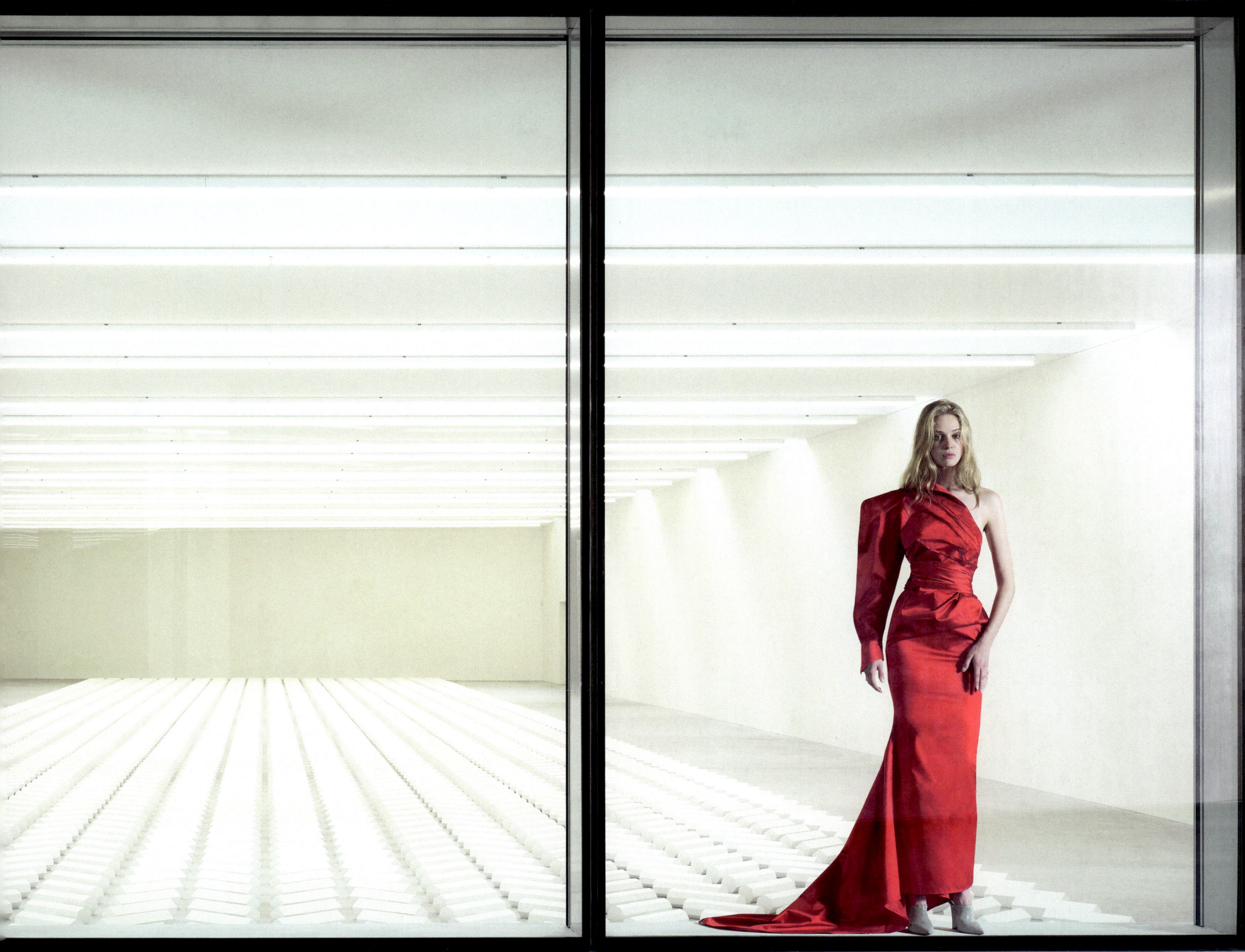

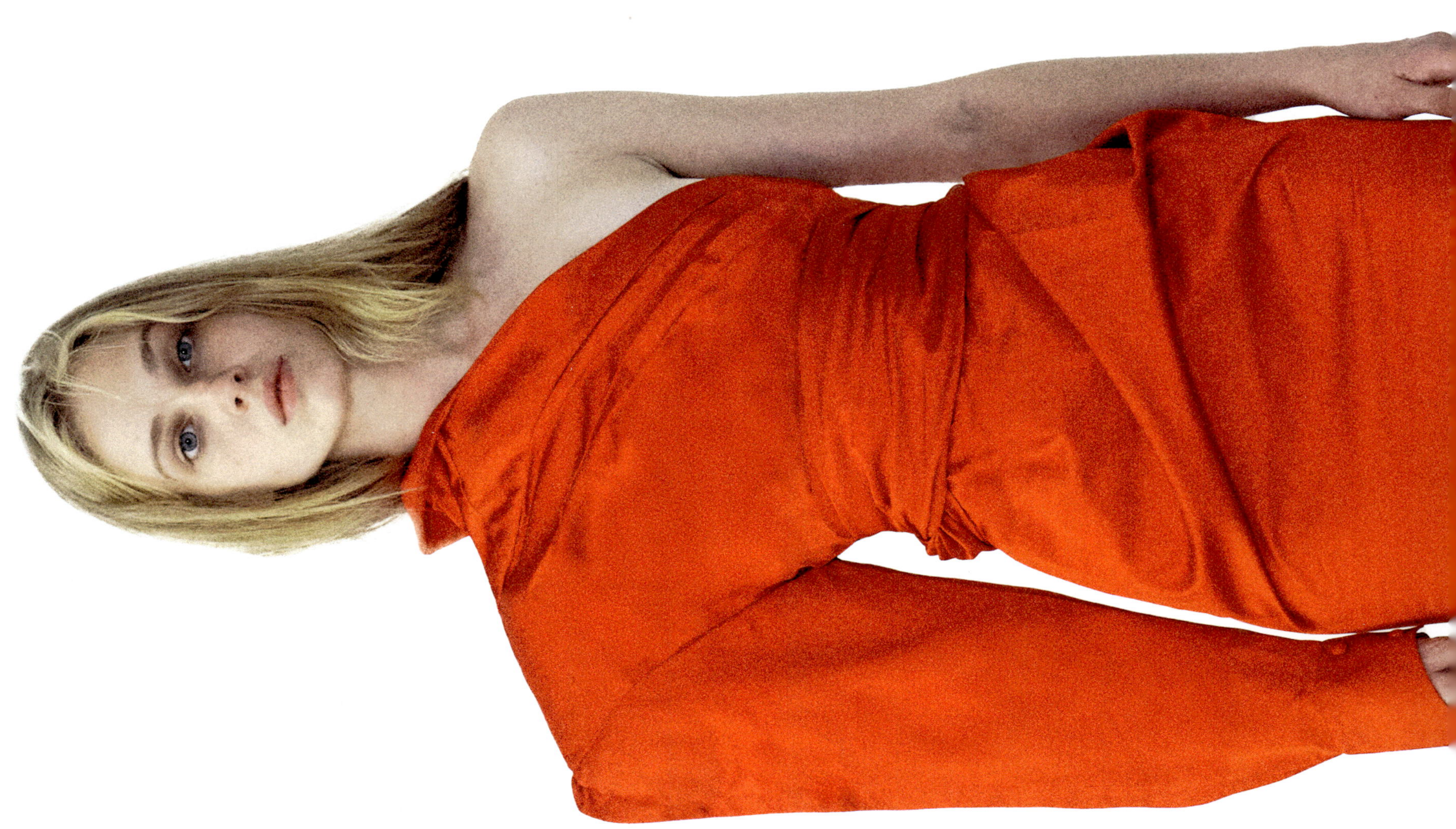

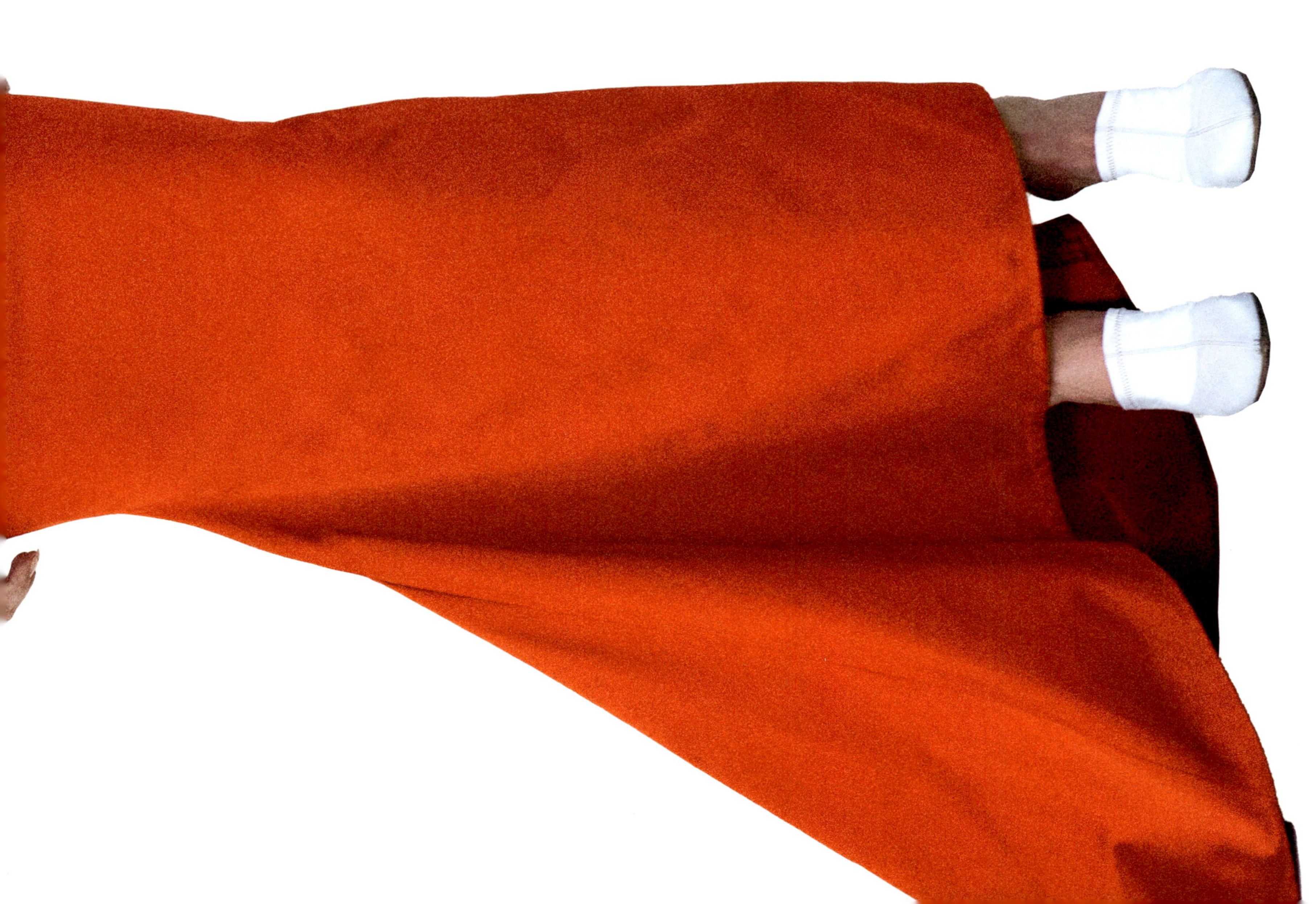

As a 1980s Dior progeny, Thierry Mugler's obsession with classical 20th-century femininity was heavily influenced by a contemporary vogue of parody and power. This gown from the *Embarquement immédiat* (Immediate Boarding) Fall/Winter 1987/88 collection celebrates the classical 1950s synched waistline while humorously reversing the cowl neckline from décolletage to back. Here, the luscious black velvet is cut with a deep rolling scoop that exposes both the subject's skin and its own pink satin lining. Cradled within are satin flowers, blooming from the lower black. The body photosynthesizing a baroque glamour. ML

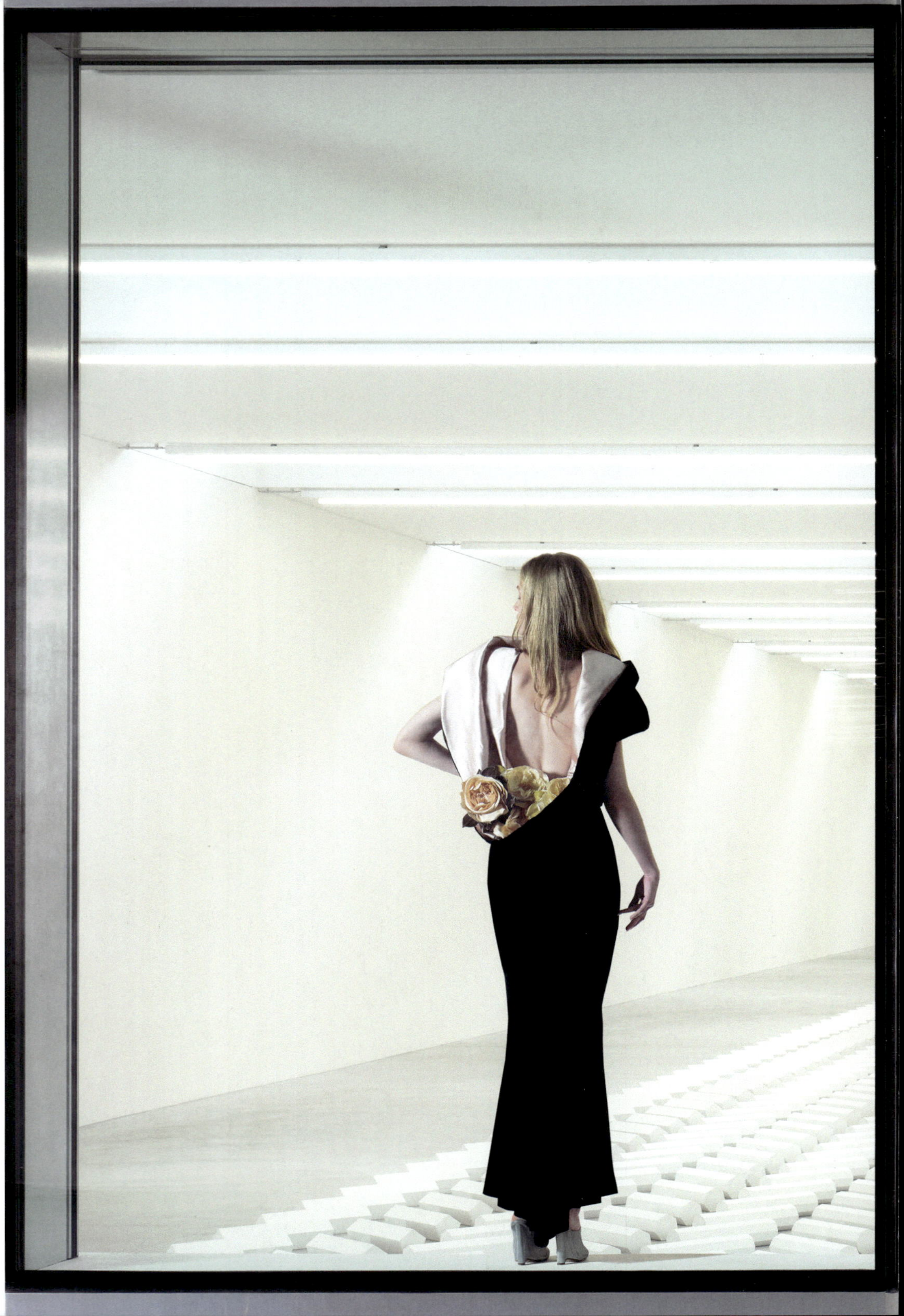

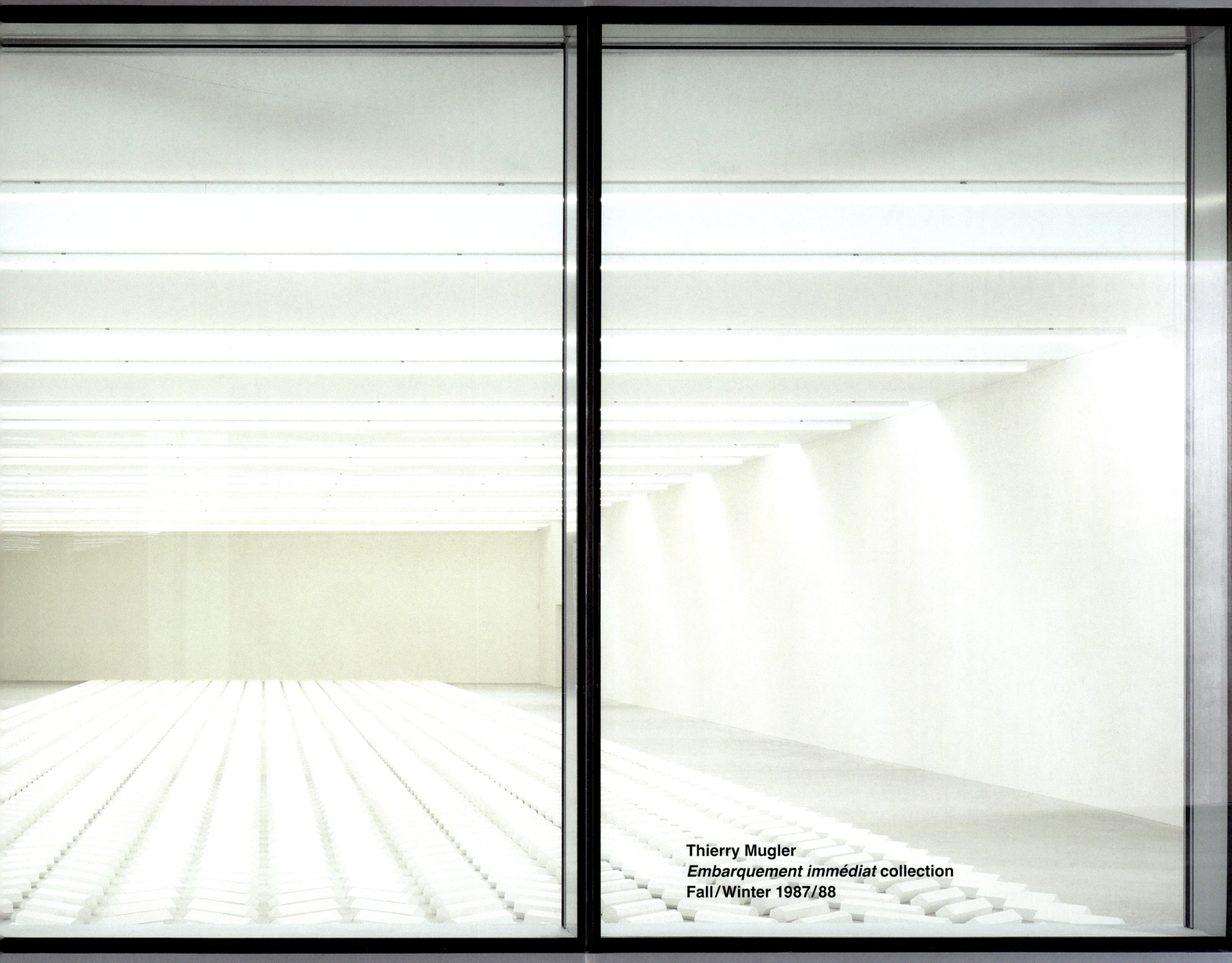

Thierry Mugler
Embarquement immédiat collection
Fall/Winter 1987/88

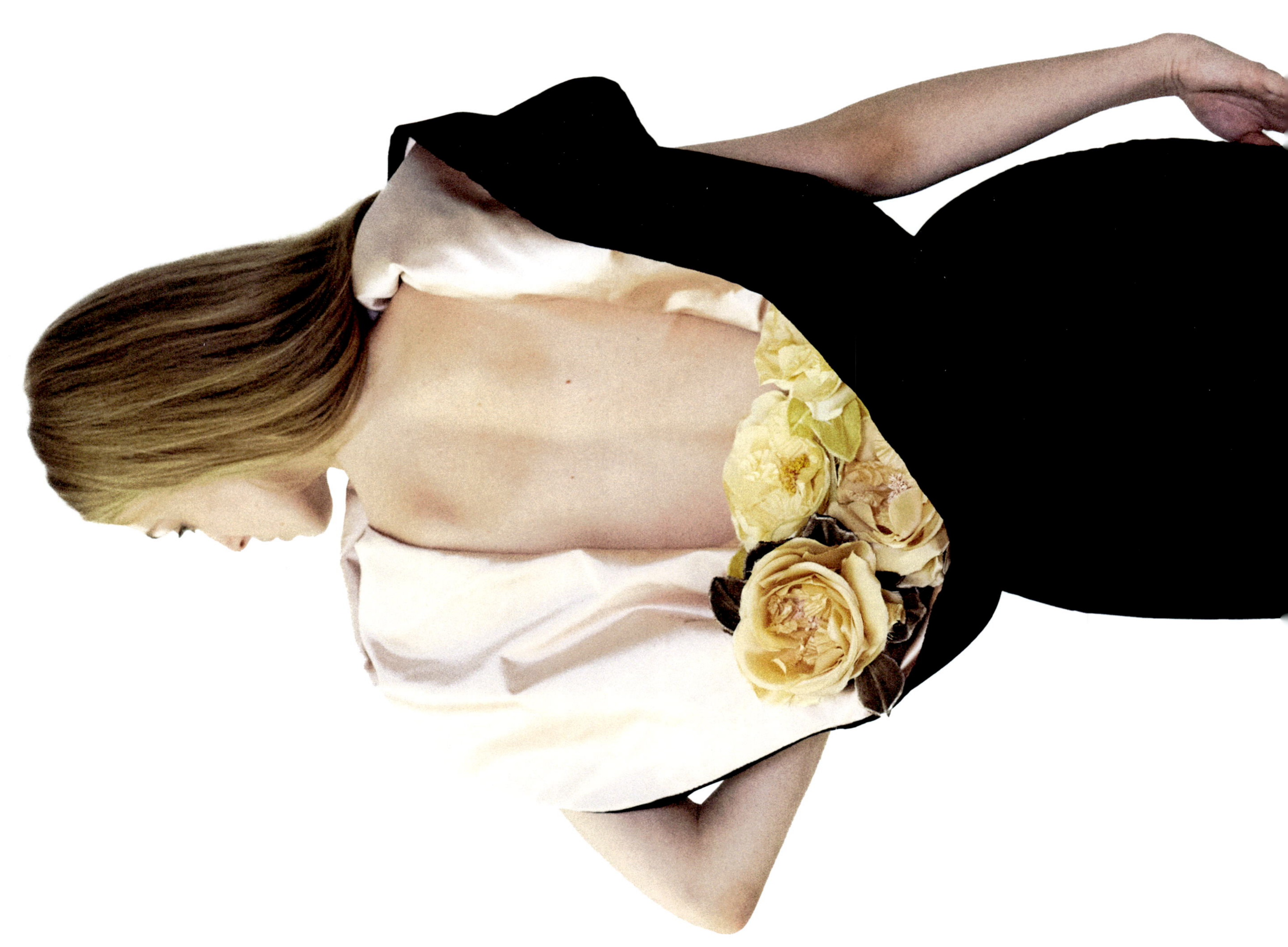

The 2000s heralded an era of corporate collusion between fast fashion retailers and their couture counterparts—a trend that saw Uniqlo, H&M, and Target commission capsule collections with designers such as Alexander McQueen, Karl Lagerfeld, Comme des Garçons, and Rodarte. The Spring/Summer 1991 collection by Alaïa, in collaboration with French discount store Tati, could then be understood as a presage for fashion history's approaching lane merge of High and Main Street. Using the chain's blown-up houndstooth insignia, Alaïa produced a figure-hugging capsule of hot pants, jackets, tops, gloves, tops, and flat caps in red, white, black, and blue. No wonder this "democratization" of fashion took the image of a valley girl: an avatar of shopping mall chic. Imagine this worn by the computer game Sims, a skin available for the popular girl. Cher Horowitz's digital wardrobe with an MS Paint fill bucket of striped checkers. The skin's only customization is scale and a limited colorway. Fashion once again narrating the amusing dialectics of uniform shopping. ML

Alaïa
Spring/Summer 1991

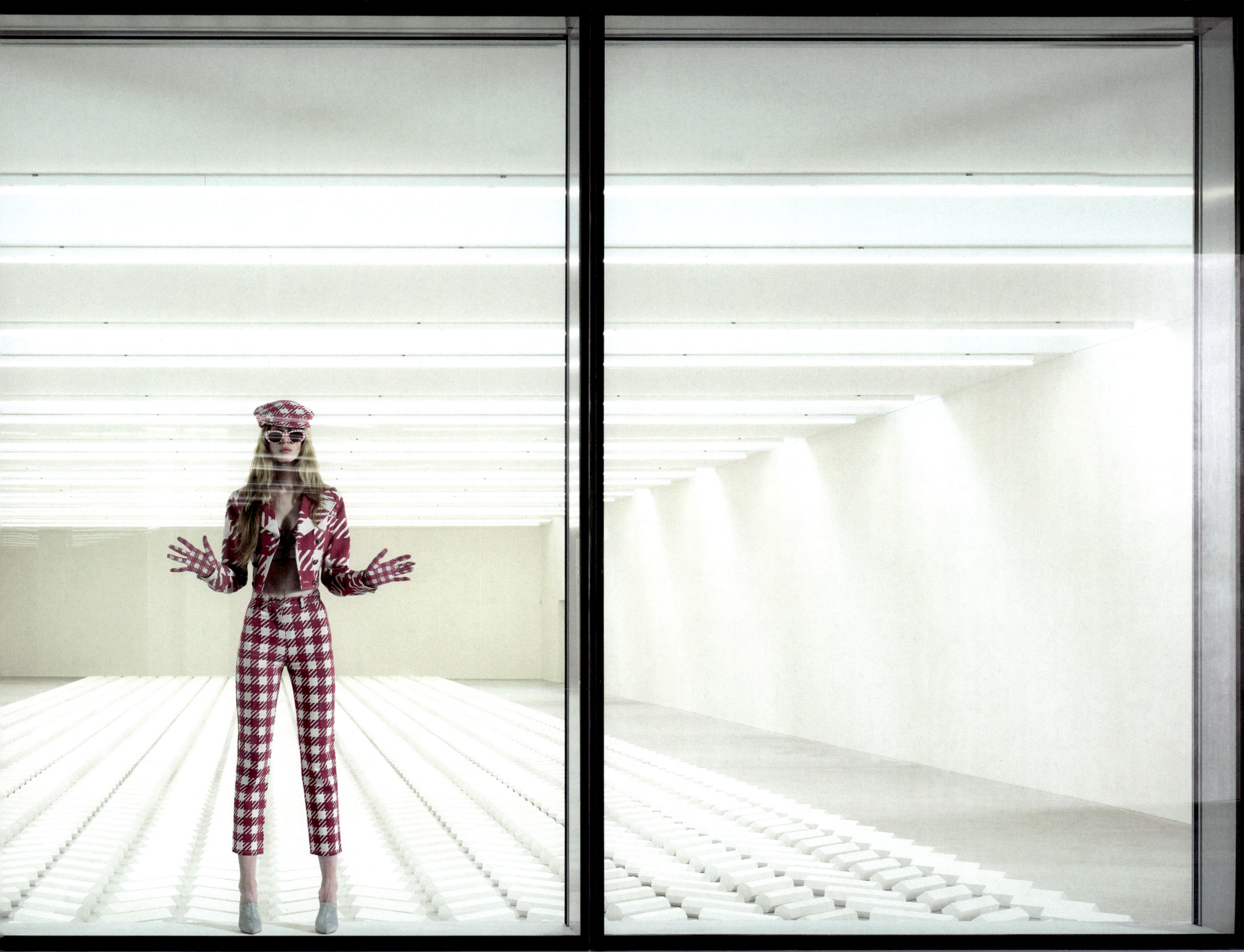

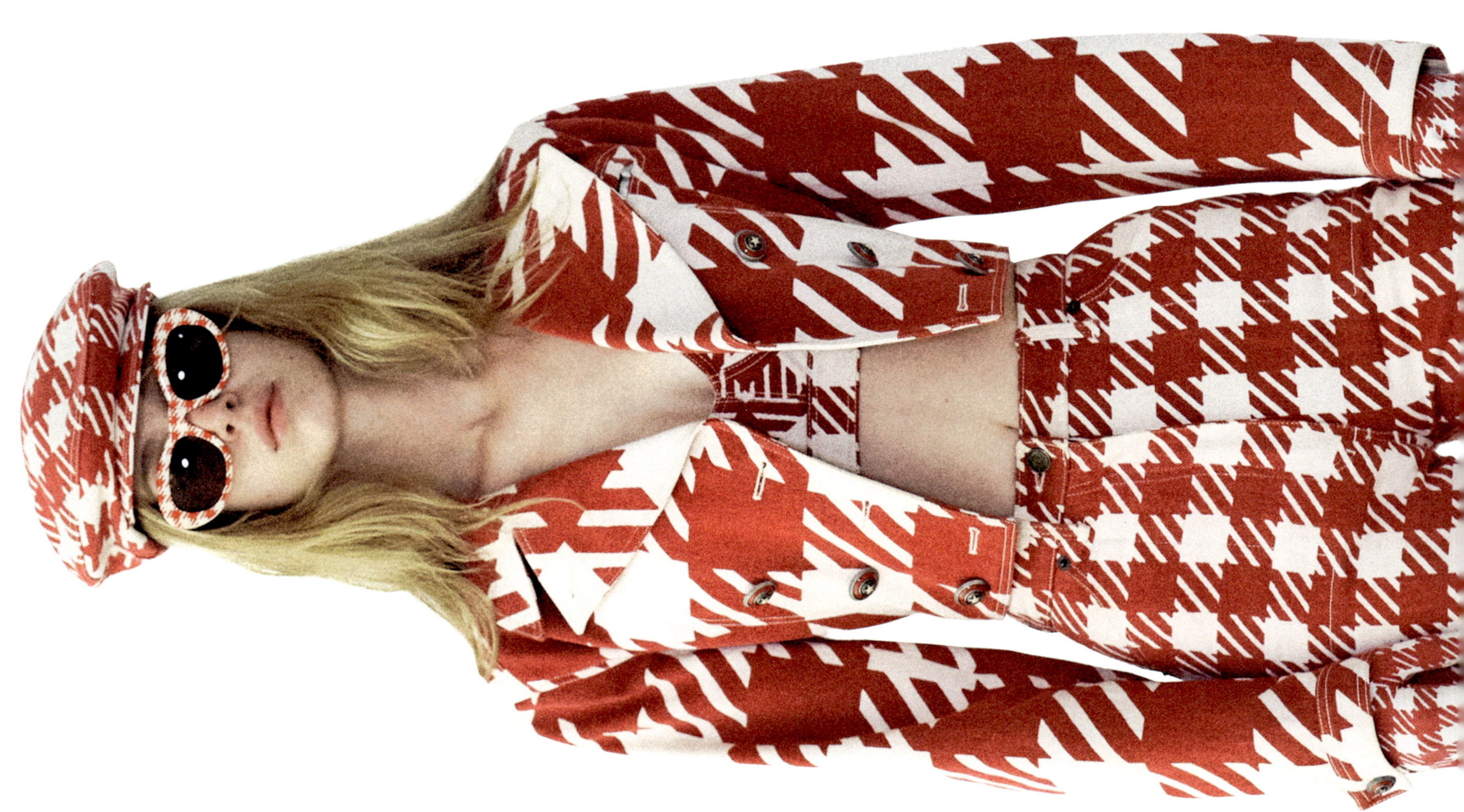

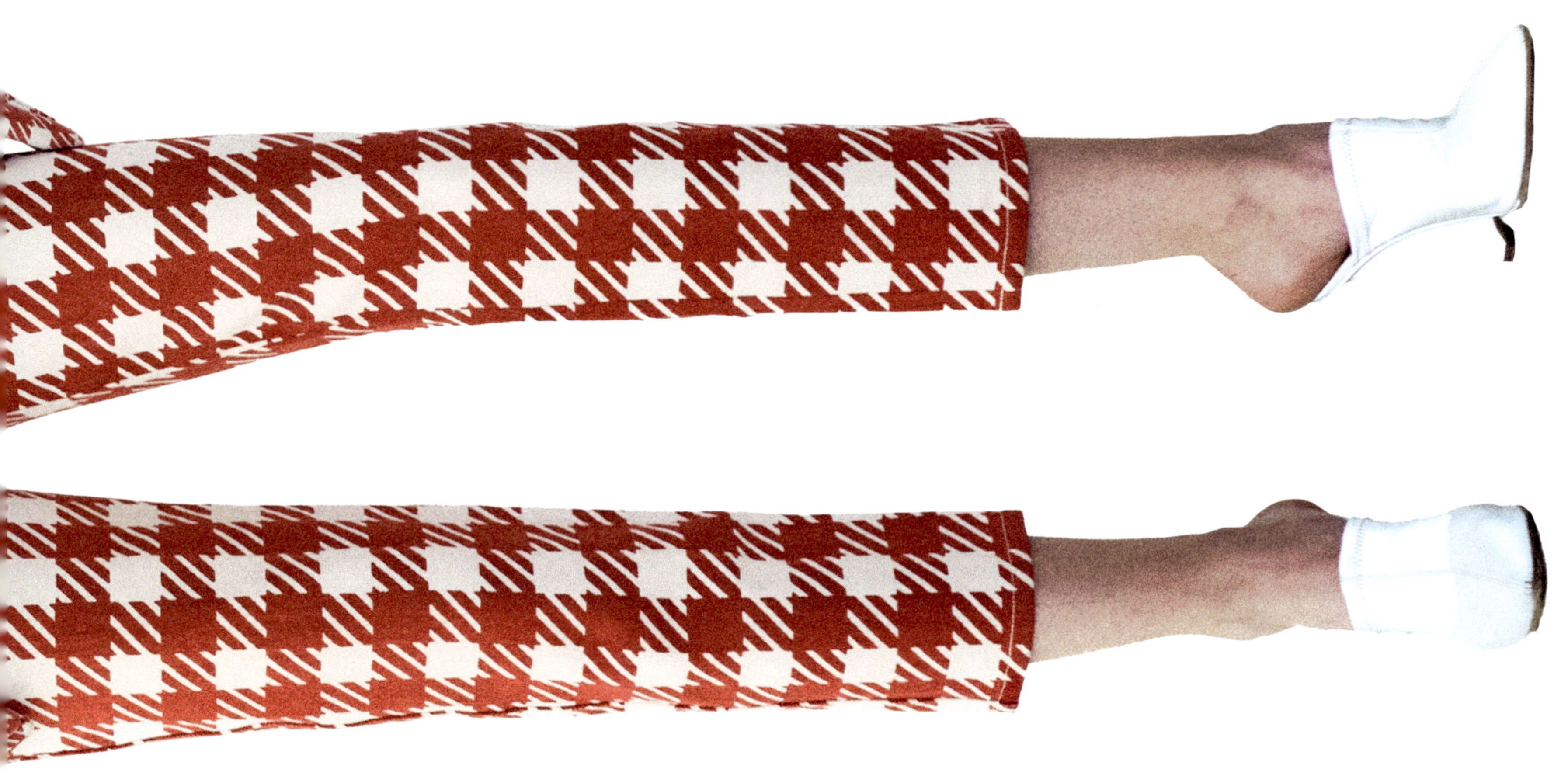

A matching long-sleeve cropped top with Bardot neckline and waisted mini-skirt in thick, black cotton blend jersey are heavily embellished with gemstones of various colors and shapes. Sporting an exposed midriff, this ensemble from Fall/Winter 1991/92 typifies Dolce & Gabbana's body-con sex appeal, black lingerie beginnings, and baroque Italian lucre. Featuring the nineties supermodels like Linda Evangelista and Naomi Campbell, the show cemented itself as a D&G classic of festive ostentation. Once again wealth manages to reassert itself. ML

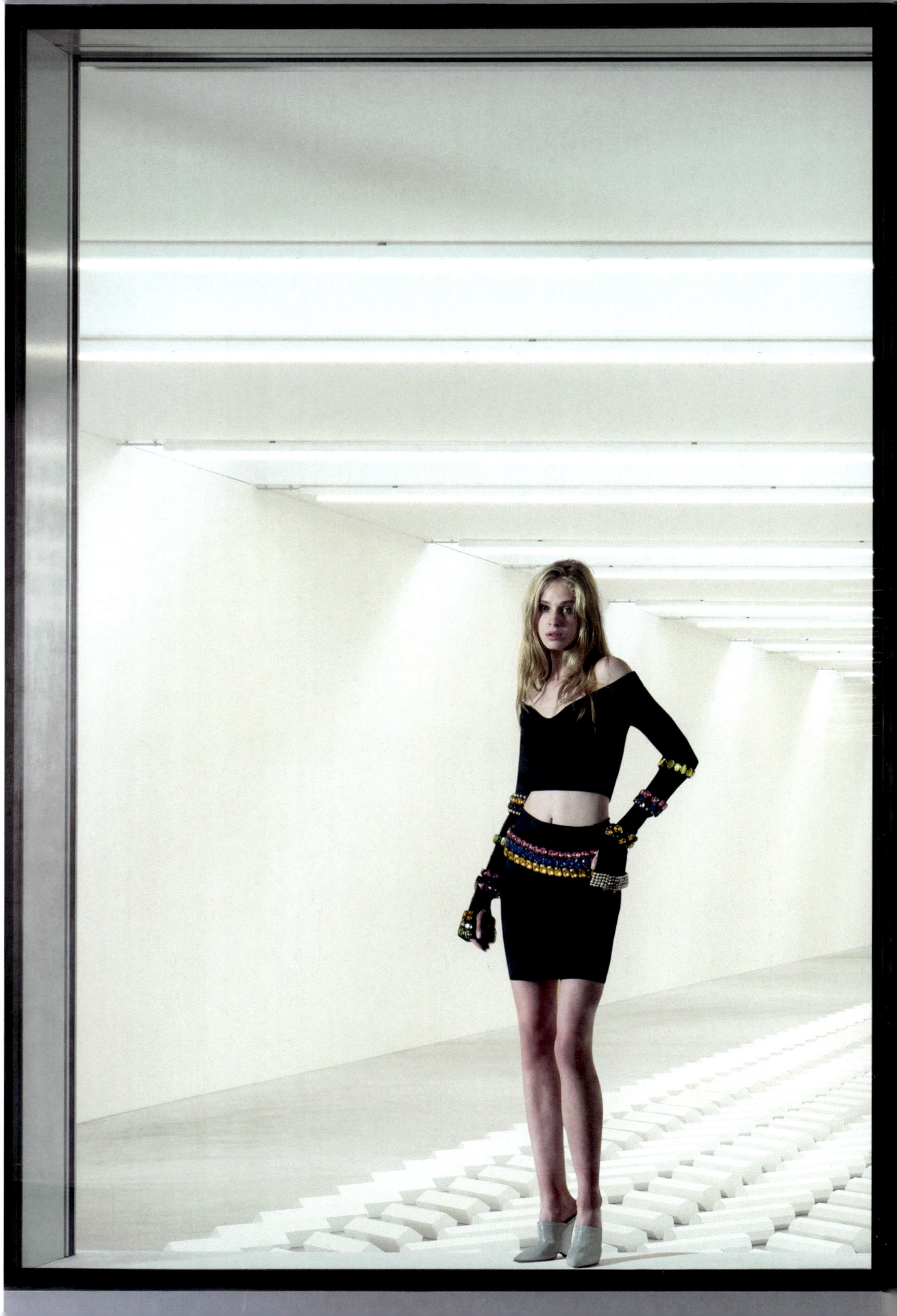

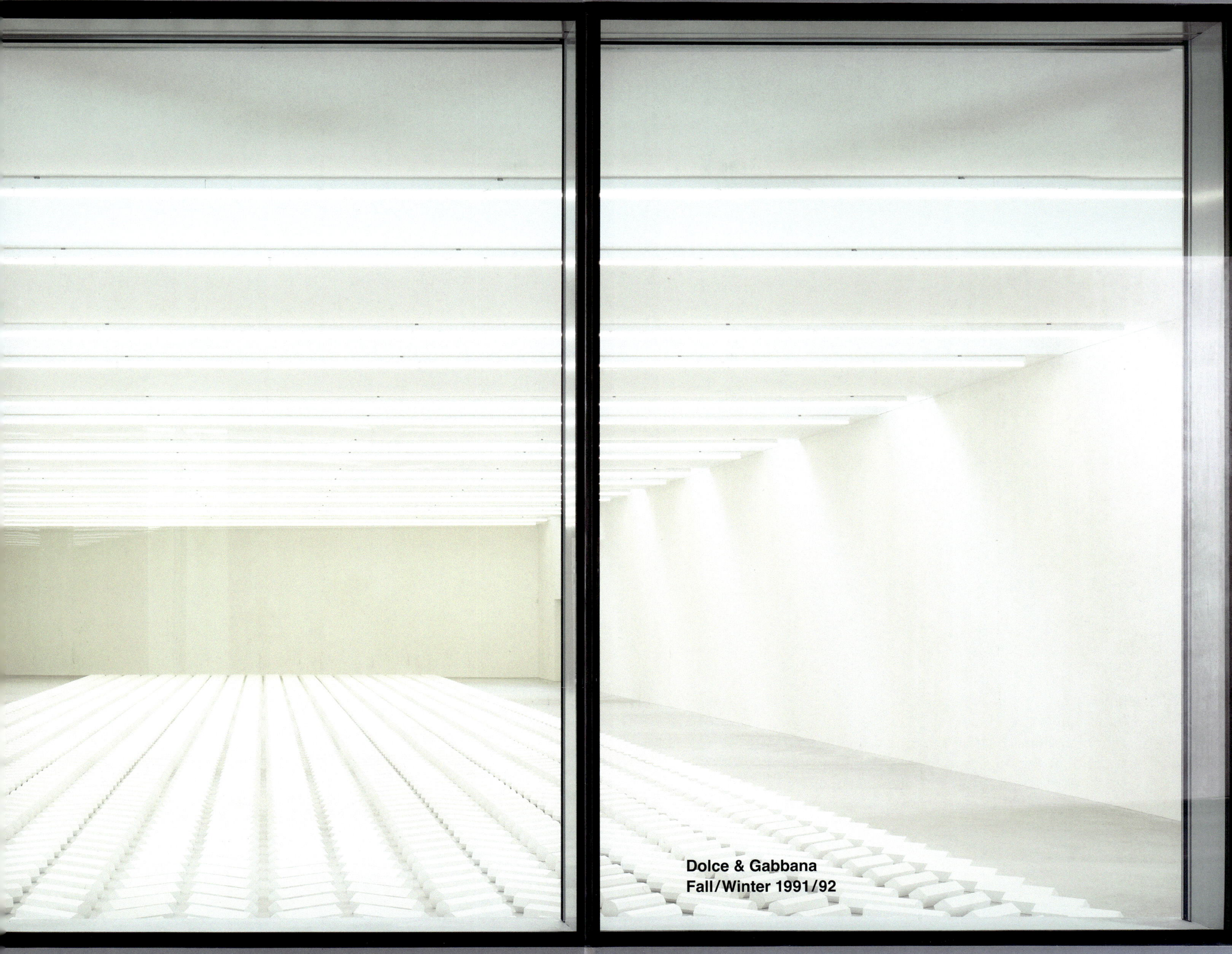
Dolce & Gabbana
Fall/Winter 1991/92

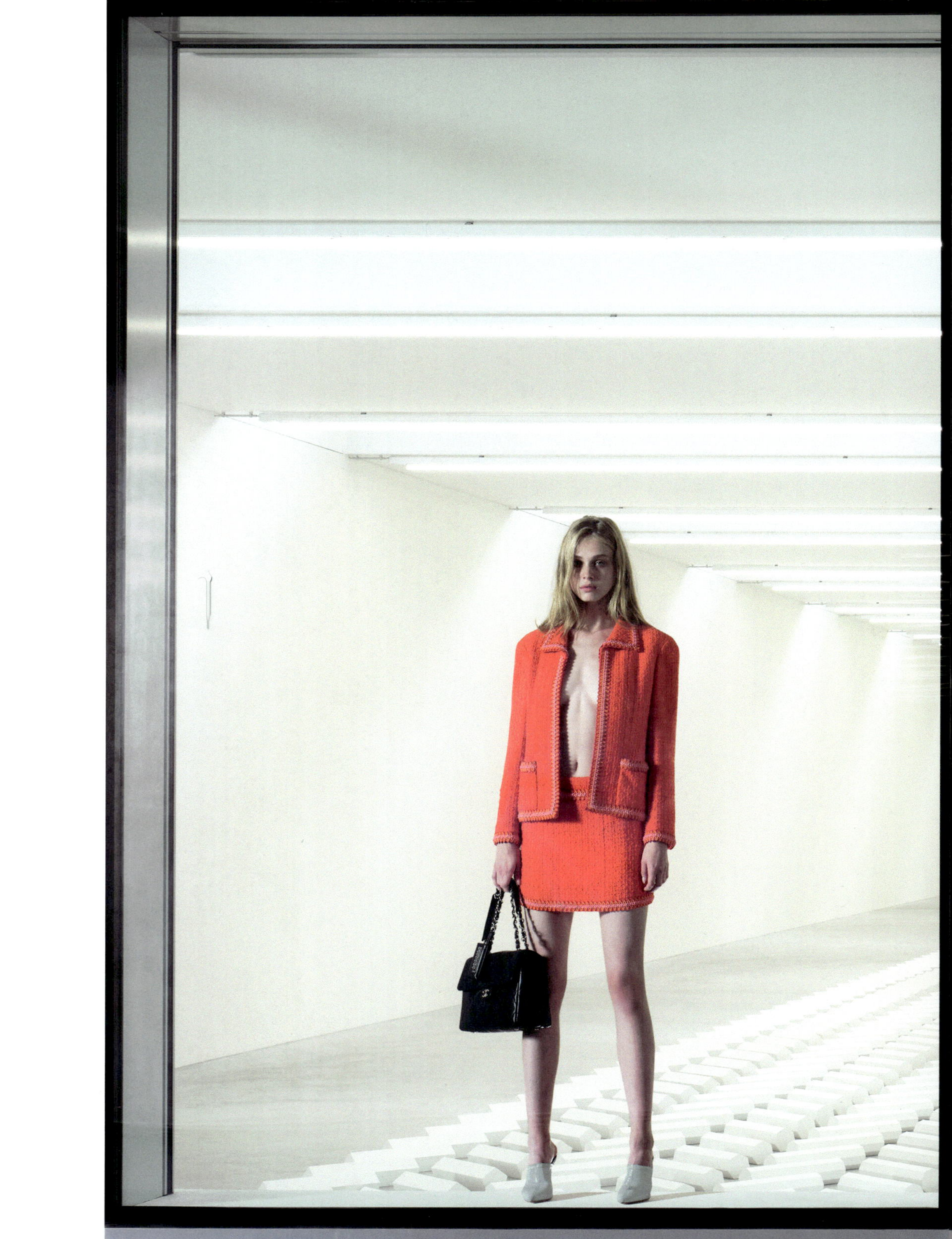

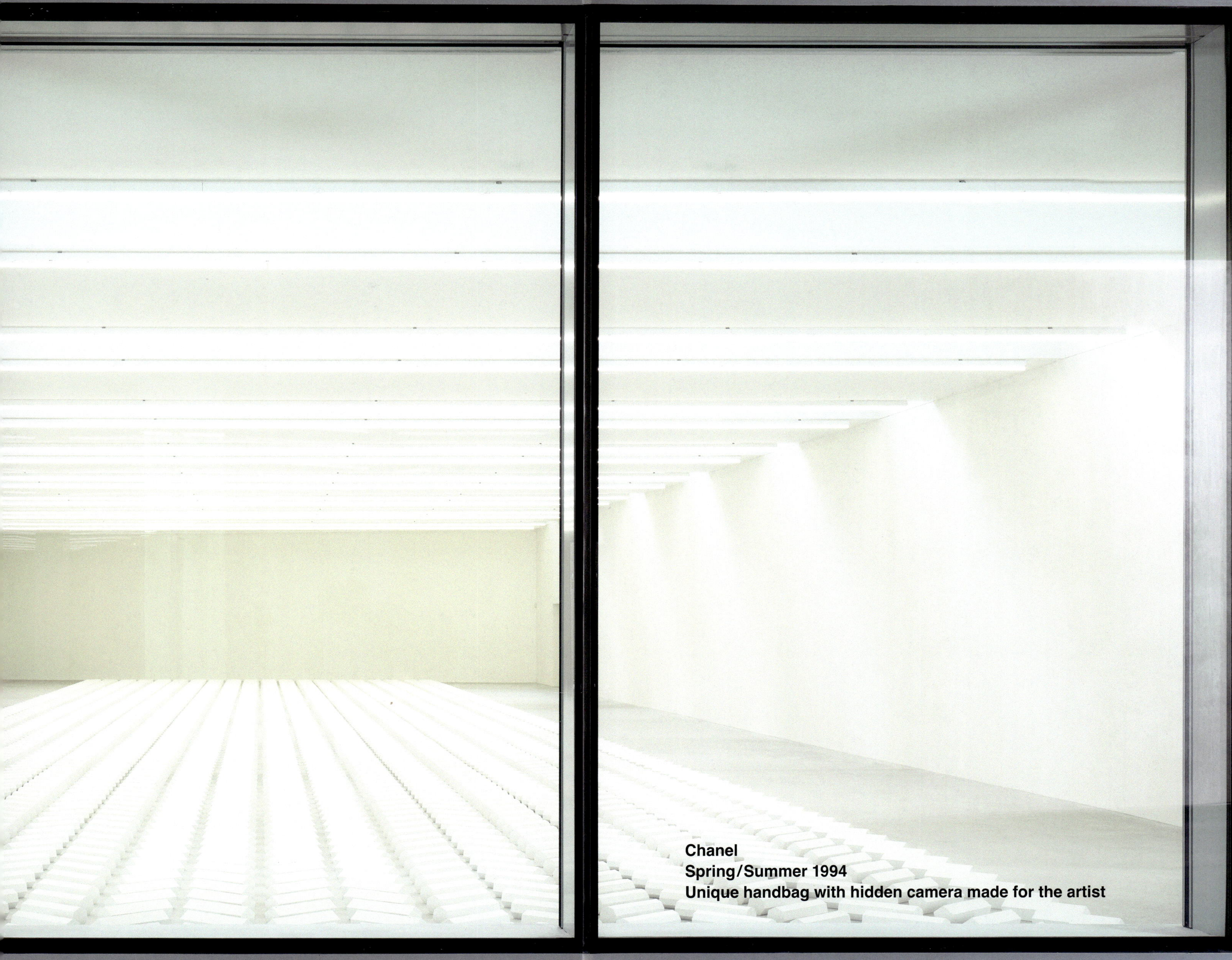

Chanel
Spring/Summer 1994
Unique handbag with hidden camera made for the artist

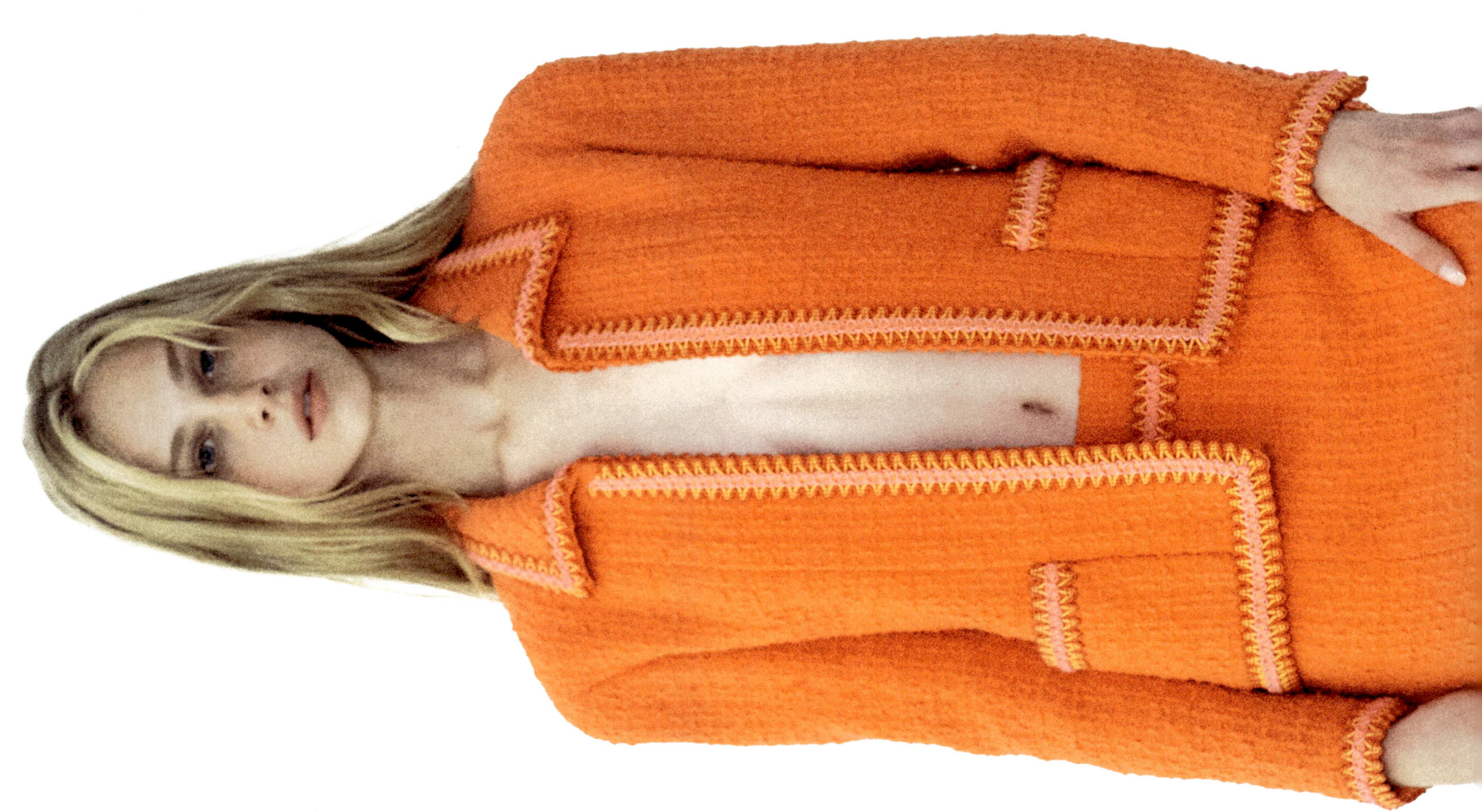

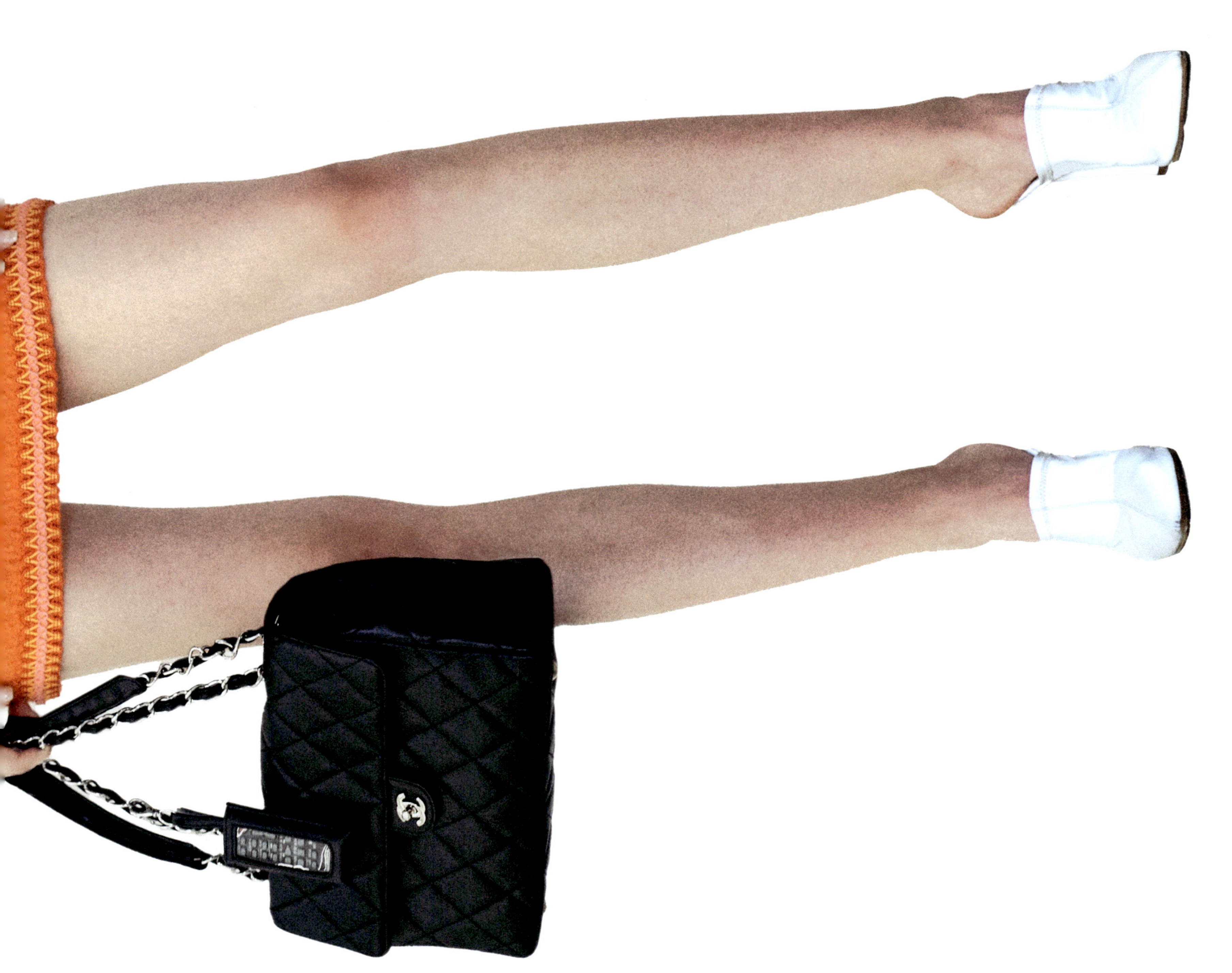

Photograph by Studio Flusser, Tchibo warehouse in West Bohemia, 2019. This work is part of the exhibition and book *Steel Cities: The Architecture of Logistics in Central and Eastern Europe* by Kateřina Frejlachová, Miroslav Pazdera, Tadeáš Říha, and Martin Špičák, 2020, courtesy of the authors.

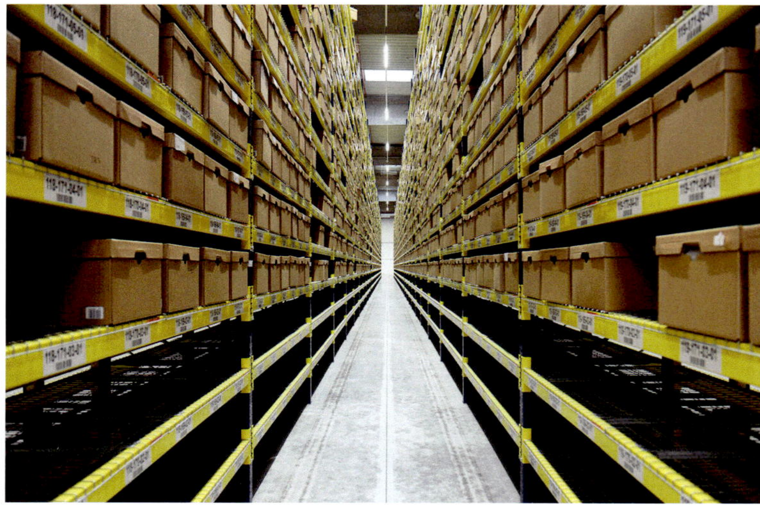

Merlin Carpenter, *Make Your Own Life*, 2006. Shopping bags and receipts.

"Merlin Carpenter asked the ICA Philadelphia, the original venue for this exhibition, to provide him with $4,000 cash. After some difficulty this was handed over a few days before the show opened. Neither the curator nor the ICA were told what the money was for. The artist then went on a wild shopping spree enjoying luxurious goods and services, with only the receipts and empty shopping bags exhibited. This project had nothing to do with Cologne."

"MAKE YOUR OWN LIFE: Artists In & Out of Cologne" was curated by Bennett Simpson and organized by and first shown at the Institute of Contemporary Art, University of Pennsylvania, Philadelphia, from April 21st to July 31st, 2006. It then toured to Toronto, Seattle, and Miami. Above is the wall text.

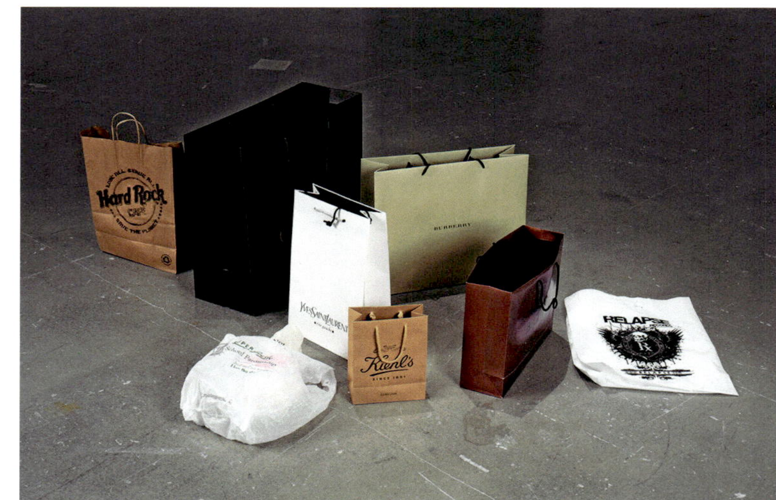

Storage at the RISD Museum at the time Andy Warhol made his selections for *Raid the Icebox 1*, 1969, courtesy of the Museum of Art, Rhode Island School of Design, Providence.

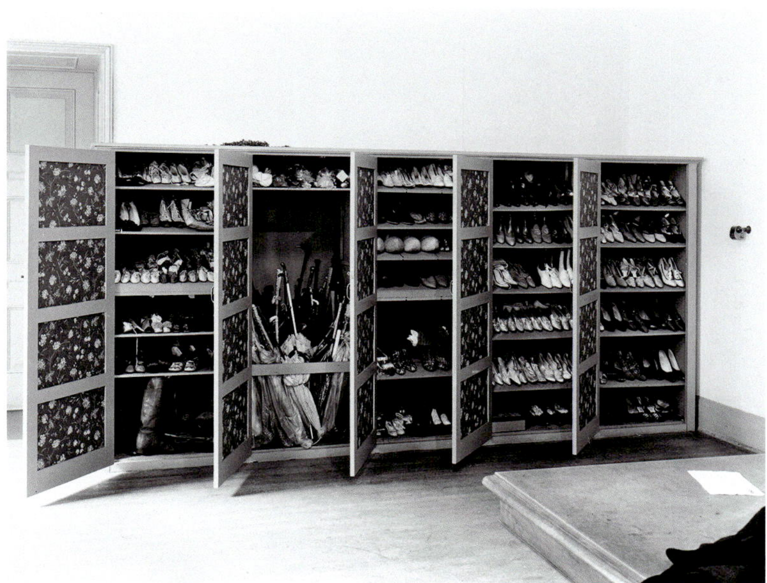

Sylvie Fleury, *Walking on Carl Andre*, 1997, film still, courtesy of the artist.

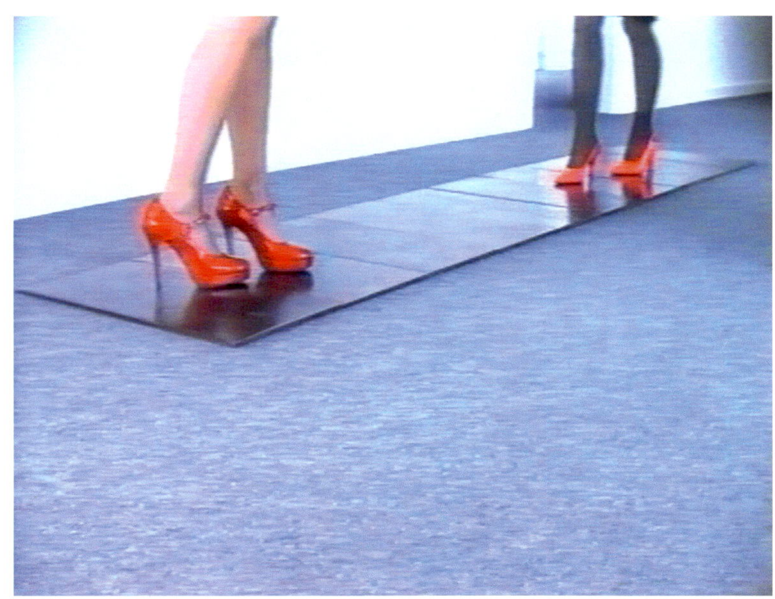

Note to the Reader

Sylvie Fleury created her site-specific exhibition *Double Positive* (2022) in response to the setting of the newly opened building of the Bechtler Stiftung, where *The 2000 Sculpture* (1992) by Walter de Maria is on permanent display. It is a site of contemplation, which is currently confronted with a provocative and unsettling encounter: Fleury's installation of numerous garment racks containing her entire wardrobe of the past three decades.

Upon arrival, we are faced with a display that looks more like a storage facility or a fashion outlet than a museum. We find ourselves wondering if the recent residential and cultural development of the estate, arrayed with several outdoor works of art, has reverted to its former industrial use. A closer look reveals quite the contrary: the humble clothes racks are gloriously aglow and the garments on view are wildly eccentric. High-fashion items give insight into the 1990 fashion avant-garde, into the days of Thierry Mugler, Vivienne Westwood, and Jean Paul Gaultier. The accumulated relics of consumerism have been transformed into historical objects worthy of display in a museum. This artist book of the same name is part of the exhibition. Annotated by the fashion historian Matthew Linde, it takes us back to Fleury's beginnings as an artist, recalling her first work from 1991: shopping bags, unopened and filled with freshly acquired luxury products displayed as a readymade sculpture. Archival portraits of the artist at work (see p. 88) are as unlikely as her "sculpture"; assuming the role of a consumer, she challenges the notion of the artist as a worker and producer.

In her installation, Fleury debunks the tenets of the predominantly male art establishment with inimitable verve. Seen through the lens of Minimal Art, the traces of a personal biography become a vulnerable act of self-exposure. For once, Fleury does not cite Mondrian, Fontana or Gober; her title alludes to Michael Heizer's *Double Negative* from 1969: land art consisting of two enormous trenches dug into the Nevada desert. Heizer's work is about the displacement of material—240,000 tons of desert sandstone—and the resulting negative space; Walter de Maria's large-scale installation is similarly overwhelming in volume, covering 500 square meters of museum space with standardized plaster rods. Fleury's *Double Positive* with numerous racks of identical generic black garment bags aesthetically mirrors the neighboring *The 2000 Sculpture*.

Prior to the exhibition, Fleury borrowed the space of de Maria's sculpture and converted it into a venue for a fashion shoot. The museum window became a show window where model Katrina Roelle paraded the clothes that stylist Ursina Gysi had selected from the artist's collection. Within the context of art in industrial spaces and the minimalism of Heizer or de Maria, Fleury presents us with yet another reinterpretation of an existing space. Her subversive take does not upgrade former industrial premises into a museum, but in fact suggests the reverse direction. In *Double Positive*, Sylvie Fleury's point of departure is the museum as a green screen for fashion shows, digital lookbooks, shopping malls or even as a post-human, e-commerce storage facility.

Fredi Fischli & Niels Olsen
Curators of Sylvie Fleury's *Double Positive*

About Bechtler Stiftung

The Bechtler Stiftung, an exhibition venue in Uster that opened in May 2022, houses Walter de Maria's *The 2000 Sculpture* (1992) and the video installation *I Couldn't Agree With You More* (1999) by Pipilotti Rist. It is run by the Walter A. Bechtler-Stiftung and is part of the Zellweger Park area. Twice a year, parallel to the two permanently exhibited installations, the Bechtler Stiftung presents temporary exhibitions of contemporary art.

The large hall, which is the centerpiece of the Bechtler Stiftung, was designed specifically for *The 2000 Sculpture*. The concrete floor slab, cast in one piece, provides a seamless ground for the 2000 diagonally arranged plaster elements. A series of cubic skylights casts natural light into the hall that changes constantly throughout the day and according to weather conditions.

The first temporary exhibition *All Chemie. Sigmar Polke and Pamela Rosenkranz*, featuring photographs by Sigmar Polke and paintings and objects by Pamela Rosenkranz, was curated by Bice Curiger and ran from May to September 2022.

In 1955, Walter A. Bechtler established the foundation of the same name. Committed to contemporary visual art throughout his life, he was active as a collector and a member of various committees of the Kunsthaus Zürich. The cultivation of art in public space was a special concern of his. He and his brother Hans were instrumental in establishing the Alberto Giacometti Foundation, which is housed in the Kunsthaus Zürich and owns the world's largest collection of works by Alberto Giacometti. After Walter A. Bechtler's death, his sons Ruedi Bechtler and Thomas Bechtler continued to develop the foundation and gave larger, more complex works to various museums on permanent loan.

In 2003, Ruedi and Thomas Bechtler laid the foundation stone for the Bechtler Stiftung with the conversion of the former Zellweger Park industrial site in Uster. Divided into five construction sites, more than 300 rental apartments were built between 2012 and 2020, executed by the architectural firms Herzog & de Meuron, Gigon/Guyer, EM2N Architekten, and Pfister Schiess Tropeano. In Zellweger Park, Ruedi and Thomas Bechtler have collaborated with internationally relevant artists to create an impressive collection of striking artworks accessible all year round. Works by Sol LeWitt, Victor Vasarely, Tadashi Kawamata, Fischli/Weiss, Lutz & Guggisberg, and the Swiss historical artist Richard Kissling can be discovered here on an area of some 100,000 square meters.

Anaïs von Holleben-Peiser
Director, Bechtler Stiftung

This book is published on the occasion of the exhibition
Double Positive by Sylvie Fleury held at the Bechtler Stiftung, Uster,
from October 8, 2022, to March 19, 2023.

Bechtler Stiftung
Weiherweg 1
8610 Uster – Switzerland
www.bechtlerstiftung.ch

Editors
Fredi Fischli & Niels Olsen

Authors
Matthew Linde, Fredi Fischli, Niels Olsen, and Anaïs von Holleben-Peiser

Photographer
Marc Asekhame

Stylist
Ursina Gysi

Costume
Lisa Preissle

Model
Katrina Roelle, Visage Agency, Zurich

Casting
Jane Morineau

Graphic Design
Teo Schifferli

Copyediting
Catherine Schelbert

Proofreading
Elizabeth MacFadyen

Typeface
Helvetica

Color Separation & Print
Druckerei Odermatt AG, Dallenwil, Switzerland

Printed in Switzerland.

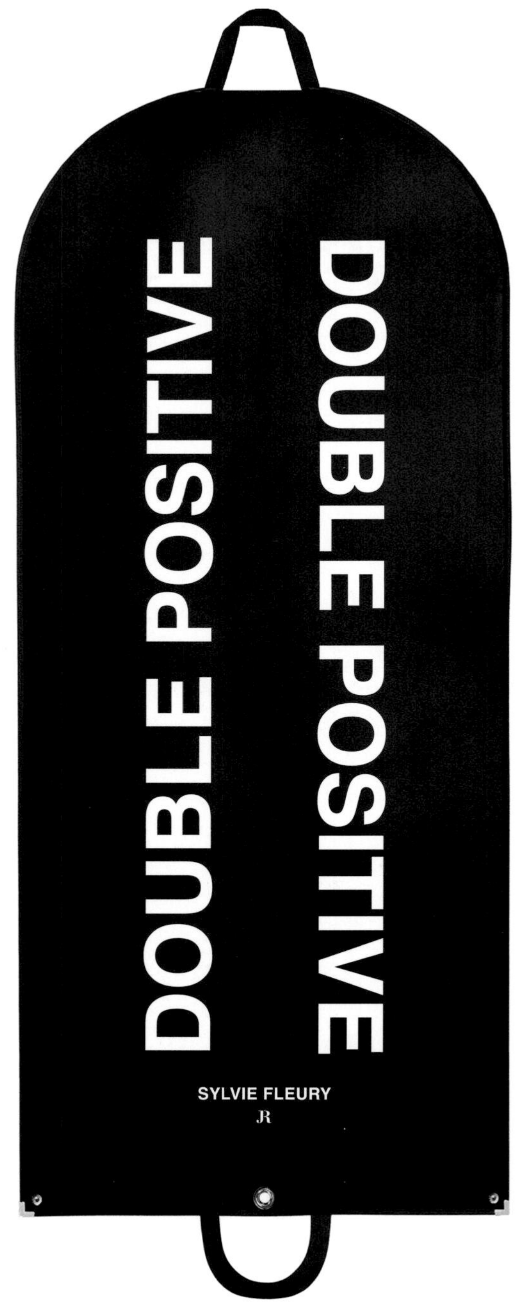

Published by

JRP|Editions
Rue des Bains, 39
CH–1205 Geneva
www.jrp-editions.com

ISBN 978-3-03764-598-7

JRP|Editions publications are available internationally at selected bookstores and from the following distribution partners:

Switzerland
AVA Verlagsauslieferung AG
avainfo@ava.ch
www.ava.ch

Germany and Austria
By JRP|Editions
info@jrp-editions.com
www.jrp-editions.com

France
Les presses du réel
info@lespressesdureel.com
www.lespressesdureel.com

UK and other European countries
Cornerhouse Publications, HOME
publications@cornerhouse.org
www.cornerhousepublications.org

USA, Canada, Asia and Australia
ARTBOOK|D.A.P.
orders@dapinc.com
www.artbook.com

For a list of our partner bookshops or for any general questions, please contact JRP|Editions directly at info@jrp-editions.com, or visit our homepage www.jrp-editions.com for further information about our program.

Sylvie Fleury, wearing a piece from the Alaïa Spring/Summer 1991 collection, installing her work in the 1991 group exhibition *No Man's Time* at Villa Arson in Nice.

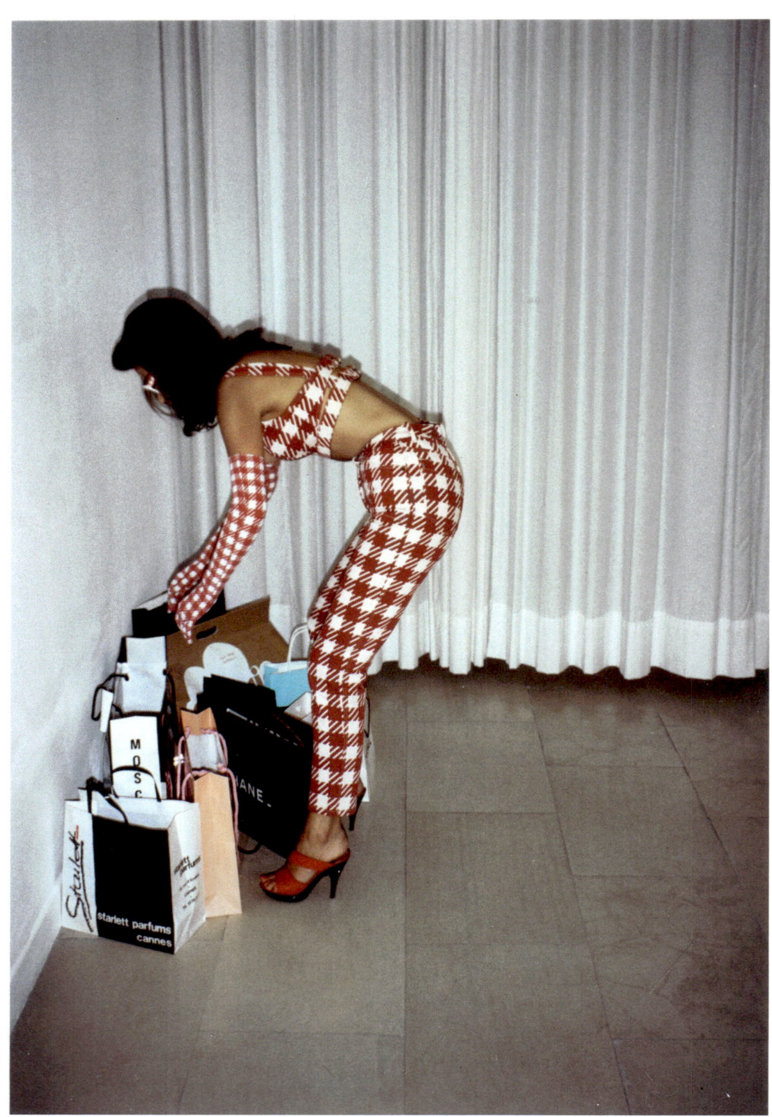